CONCILIUM

CONCILIUM
ADVISORY COMMITTEE

Gregory Baum	Montreal/QC. Canada
José Oscar Beozzo	São Paulo, SP Brazil
Wim Beuken	Louvain, Belgium
Leonardo Boff	Petrópolis, Brazil
John Coleman	Los Angeles, CA. USA
Norbert Greinacher	Tübingen, Germany
Gustavo Gutiérrez	Lima, Peru
Hermann Häring	Tübingen, Germany
Werner G. Jeanrond	Oslo, Norway
Jean-Pierre Jossua	Paris, France
Maureen Junker-Kenny	Dublin, Ireland
François Kabasele Lumbala	Kinshasa, Rep. Dem. Congo
Nicholas Lash	Cambridge, UK
Mary-John Mananzan	Manila, The Philippines
Alberto Melloni	Reggio, Emilia Italy
Norbert Mette	Münster, Germany
Dietmar Mieth	Tübingen, Germany
Jürgen Moltmann	Tübingen, Germany
Teresa Okure	Port Harcourt, Nigeria
Aloysius Pieris	Kelaniya/Colombo, Sri Lanka
Giuseppe Ruggieri	Catania, Italy
Paul Schotsmans	Louvain, Belgium
Janet Martin Soskice	Cambridge, UK
Elsa Tamez	San José, Costa Rica
Christoph Theobald	Paris, France
David Tracy	Chicago, Ill. USA
Marciano Vidal	Madrid, Spain
Ellen van Wolde	Tilburg, The Netherlands
Johannes Zizioulas	Pergamo, Turkey
Regina Ammicht Quinn	Tübingen Germany
Hille Haker	Chicago, USA
Jon Sobrino	San Salvador, El Salvador
Luiz Carlos Susin	Porto Alegre, Brazil
Silvia Scatena	Bologna, Italy
Susan A. Ross	USA, Los Angeles
Solange Lefebvre	Montreal/QC. Canada
Erik Borgman	Amsterdam, Netherlands
Andres Torres Queiruga	Santiago, Spain

CONCILIUM   2020/1

Decolonial Theology:
Violence, Resistance and Spiritualities

Edited by

Edited by Carlos Mendoza-Álvarez and
Thierry-Marie Courau

Published in 2019 by SCM Press, 3rd Floor, Invicta House, 108–114 Golden Lane, London EC1Y 0TG.

SCM Press is an imprint of Hymns Ancient & Modern Ltd (a registered charity) 13A Hellesdon Park Road, Norwich NR6 5DR, UK

Copyright © International Association of Conciliar Theology, Madras (India)

www.concilium.in

English translations copyright © 2020 Hymns Ancient & Modern Ltd.

All rights reserved. No part of this publication may be reproduced, stored in a retrieval system, or transmitted, in any form or by any means, electronic, mechanical, photocopying or otherwise, without the prior written permission of the Board of Directors of Concilium.

ISBN 978-0-334-05956-1

Concilium is published in March, June, August, October, December

Contents

Editorial

Part One: Violence

Accumulation Through Robbery and Systemic Violence
RAÚL ZIBECHI   12

Transitions, Acts of Resistance and the Women's Movement:
A View from Colombia
GINA MARCELA ÁRIAS RODRÍGUEZ AND
LUIS ADOLFO MARTÍNEZ HERRERA   23

Part Two: Resistance

Care for the Common Home
GUSTAVO ESTEVA FIGUEROA   35

Women in Their Various Struggles: Spiritual Activism as
'Other' Knowledge
SUSAN ABRAHAM   46

Part Three: Spiritualities

Relational Wisdom and Spiritualities in Abya Yala
SOFÍA CHIPANA QUISPE   59

Theology of the Quilombo: Afro-Brazilian Spiritual Resistance
CLEUSA CALDEIRA   69

Diverse Communities Inhabited by the Divine Ruah
JOSÉ DE JESÚS LEGORRETA ZEPEDA   80

Acts of Resistance: Messianic Force of Divine Anarchy
JUAN CARLOS LA PUENTE TAPIA   89

Part Four: Theological Forum

From Vatican II to the Synod on Amazonia: Towards a Synodal Church
ALFREDO FERRO MEDINA SJ   101

The Reform of the Roman Curia
AGENOR BRIGHENTI   106

In Memoriam: J.B. Metz
FRANCIS SCHÜSSLER FIORENZA   111

Contributors   115

Editorial

Postcolonial Theology

This issue presents the most significant elements that constitute a *decolonial* theology and come from dialogue with other sciences and forms of knowledge, listening to social movements and other agents of social change in these uncertain times of globalisation that thinkers from the epistemology of the South have called 'the Fourth World War'. The articles represent the wealth of various decolonial inputs made during the international Congress 'Resist! Forms of Violence, Resistance and Spirituality' held at the Universidad Iberoamericana Mexico City and the Centro Universitario Cultural, from 28 to 30 May 2019.

We set out here three stages of analysis presenting the elements of decolonial theology. Each of these stages is cut across by transverse voices that come, first, from the social movements that resist in various ways, then from organised civil society that supports these resistance movements, followed by academic voices as a 'rearguard' to tease out the meaning that emerges from the cracks in the wall of hegemonic thought, expressed by artists whose narratives and performances describe and act out *a different possible world*, with the aid of their creative imagination. We should remember that the voice of theology, following this decolonial path, can only stammer out redemption and the divine names under its breath, without triumphalism or new attempts to sacralise the divine if it is to speak of the loving mystery of reality that emerges out of these acts of resistance, in the midst of the ruins of hegemonic instrumental modernity.

The first stage presents a general overview of the systemic violence of the contemporary world by means of four sectoral examinations by two specialists on Latin America who describe the scene of a global systemic war with four pillars: the extractive economy, the hetero-normative patriarchy, migration in the sense of forced movement, and the return of extreme right-wing governments. Raúl Zibechi describes the basic problem of the extractivist society, explained as a network of enrichment

Editorial

through plunder that creates 'open-air surveillance mechanisms' for half of the world's population. Gina Árias and Luis Adolfo Martínez analyse the difficult construction of peace in context of war, as part of a web of diverse forms of violence in which acts of resistance by women, illustrated by the case of Colombia, set up signposts to undo the logic of the domination of territories and bodies as booty in the world's new wars.

The second stage of analysis stresses the role of social movements, involved in different forms of resistance, with standard academic and theological analysis in dialogue with other disciplines that critically analyse the practices and narratives of world change that are found across the whole planet. Gustavo Esteva's article describes the two models of care for the common home in action at this uncertain time for life on the planet: the one dictated by the hegemonic powers and the one being built, day by day, by organisations and peoples in local and regional resistance. For her part, Susan Abraham analyses the different coalitions and forms of solidarity among women as they reflect post-colonial and decolonial forms of feminism in their efforts to oppose patriarchal violence with its weight of racism, sexism, classism and other forms of discrimination, emphasising that in the epistemological South feminisms are offering new challenges if we are to build societies with gender equity and justice, based on diverse forms of wisdom.

The third stage is theological in the strict sense. It looks in more detail at the role of spiritualities – as the starting point of religious experience – when they emerge as an expression of resistance movements that face horror with dignity and hope: glimmers of a decolonial theology as illustrative of redemption taking place in the cracks and gaps in the violent history of the globalised world. Sofía Chipana's reflection, doing theology with the epistemologies of the South, talks about forms of ancestral knowledge as forms of spiritual and cognitive resistance, linked to the care for the sister mother Earth as an old and new form of American thinking through feeling. As a counterpoint from spiritualities denied, but resisting, Cleusa Caldeira's article puts its finger into the wound of epistemological and theological racism that has left the Afro-descendant peoples of Brazil and all America invisible, but which is challenged today by a black spirituality with African roots but nourished by the sap of Christian faith. As an expression of resistance movements the outlines of a decolonial ecclesiology are sketched in José Legorreta's article, which

Editorial

focuses on the treatment of the category of community by identitarian social and religious systems, now countered by new forms of sociality that call for a new 'ecclesiology of emergent communities'. And as an expression of the messianic force found in history 'from its underside', Juan Carlos La Puente offers us pointers from ancient apophatic mysticism looking towards a post-modern theological reflection on the potential of 'divine an-archy' flowing in vulnerable and wounded subjectivities, which, paradoxically, through the resilience that comes from their open wounds, shared with other system victims, live the glimmers of hope in the midst of the broken history of humanity.

The Forum is devoted to urgent ecclesiological issues, focusing on the urgent need for reform of the Catholic Church. We have a cutting review of the underlying themes of the recent Synod on Amazonia by Alfredo Ferro, and the repercussions of this synodal path begun by the Second Vatican Council but reaching down to our time, in the shape of the reform of the Vatican curia, in the erudite and wise reflection of Agenor Brighenti. Finally, as an expression of theology as the living and grateful memory of one of the founders of the review *Concilium*, an obituary by Francis Fiorenza honours the arduous work of Johannes Baptist Metz, the renowned European theologian who promoted theological reflection based on an incarnate faith, making space with all his prophetic force for a political theology from the victims in the European context of the 20th century's wars.

We are confident that these theological and interdisciplinary reflections, arising like a murmur from bodies 'thrown away as refuse' by the global hegemony, but alive with ethical and spiritual resistance and imagination, may be a source of action and narratives of dignity and hope in other contexts, always listening to and caring for the Life that is a superabundant gift for all, whatever their gender.

Carlos Mendoza-Álvarez and Thierry-Marie Courau

Translated by Francis McDonagh

Part One: Violence

Accumulation Through Robbery and Systemic Violence

RAÚL ZIBECHI

The various forms of violence that affect the peoples of Latin America are not exceptional situations, the result of the attitude of a government or a critical situation. We are facing structural forms of violence whose roots go deep into a model of society structured round accumulation through plunder, which is the form neoliberalism takes in this period. The militarisation of everyday life, organised crime and femicides have to be understood in this context and can be summed up as a war against the peoples and the poor to clear territories or to convert common property into goods for sale.

In most of the analyses that deal with the areas of critical thinking we find a tendency to cut off economics from politics, particular situations from the structures, as though they were completely separable variables, with the result that we lose the unifying thread of system in our understanding of the world. There is a reasonable consensus among critical thinkers in accepting David Harvey's argument that accumulation through plunder is the core of capital accumulation in this period of the decadence of the world-system.[1] Nevertheless we do not have analyses capable of linking the plunder of mother earth and that of those of us who live on it (the dynamic we call 'economics'), with the political system known as representative democracy, as though each was autonomous.

Something similar happens with interpretations of the various forms of violence, from femicides to massacres carried out by criminal groups, including state and para-state violence. Most often we get the impression that these cases of violence are episodic or to do with a particular situation, avoiding the possibility of considering them as an inseparable part of the capitalist world system in its current stage. In the same way we approach democracy with the belief that it is still the same system as functioned in periods before the development of accumulation by plunder. On the contrary, I believe that these analytic weaknesses are inseparable from the crisis of critical thinking and are part of it, tied as it is to its colonial and patriarchal origin in the North of the world-system. Or, as Frantz Fanon put it, it is a system of thought originating in the zone of being that claims to be applicable without modification to the zone of non-being.[2] I shall therefore try to identify some links or bridges between the different variables of present-day capitalism, with the aim of advancing in the design of analytic approaches that can account more coherently for our oppressions.

Extractivism or extractive society?
The first issue I wish to address is the appropriateness of calling the system an 'extractive society', since the concept of 'extractivism' seems tied to economics. Neither extractivism nor capitalism is an economic model. Capitalism is not an economy, although there is a capitalist economy. Extractivism is not an economy; it is societies or sets of social relations that go much further than the economy, since the include all aspects of a society.[3]

Extractivism is a model of recolonisation of our societies or an updating, with modifications, of the fact of colonialism. To develop this idea I shall mention some features of the extractivist model that appear in various analyses. In the first place, extractivism implies a vertical occupation of territories, whether through monocultures, mining or hydrocarbons. Secondly, it establishes asymmetrical relations between large transnational firms and states and populations. From a structural point of view, the main effect of extractivism has been 'to reinstall a new pattern of economic assymetries through the creation territories specialising in the provision of natural resources taken over and operated under the control of large transnational firms'.[4]

Thirdly, extractivism installed enclave economies, as happened in colonial times. These enclaves do not pour riches on to the population because they are economies focused on export, with minimal connection to their social context.[5] Extractivism is, fourthly, an attack on family agriculture and food sovereignty. In addition to the environmental consequences, especially on water, communities lose access to certain areas of production, the presence of extractivism encourages rural-urban migration and redefinition of territories as a consequence of the vertical intervention of the companies, which create local transnationalised areas.[6]

The fifth characteristic is the permanent militarisation of the territories. Extractivism goes in hand with what the Italian philosopher Giorgio Agamben calls a 'permanent state of exception'.[7] Where the extractive model is installed, laws and legal protections for the population disappear. In other words, this permanent state of exception is part of this model. One of the principal problems of this model of plunder is that it was initially administered by progressive governments, which represented deep bewilderment for the exploited and oppressed peoples of Latin America. Still worse, it came accompanied by decolonising language such as that of *Suma Qamaña, Living Well*, which even talks about defending life and nature, but does the opposite. The peoples don't get over such a blow in a couple of days. It is a new reality that has to be assimilated and understood.

As a result, it is not possible to produce merely economic alternatives to extractivism or accumulation by plunder, as its core is the concentrated power of the elites. Getting away from this model means defeating it, constructing new powers, a new culture and social relations anchored in different ways of life. In hegemonic discourse the term extractivism is used to cover what happens in the mines or the soya plantations and their effects on the environment and health.

We have to understand that the current model has destroyed the previous society; it has not just produced 'reforms', but profound mutations, opening the way for a regressive process in the distribution of land and global wealth.[8] Democracy is weakened and in extractivist areas ceases to exist; states become subordinate to the large companies to the point that the populations can no longer rely on the institutions to protect them from the multinationals. For these reasons it is not possible to abandon the current model without a crisis, but at the same time if we do not abandon it we are moving towards a set of extremely destructive crises, in politics, society, health and the environment. We are faced by a system, the nature of capitalism in its period of decadence, which includes institutions, which shows itself in the culture of acquisition and consumerism, a model that has destroyed traditional forms of sociability and has individualised human relations by making them dependent on the financial system. Extractivism is promoting a complete restructuring of societies and states in Latin America.

Accumulation by plunder or war against the peoples To understand the consequences of accumulation by plunder, it is necessary to compare it with the previous period, centred on accumulation by an expanded accumulation of capital, typical of industrial society. Unlike the old industrial model, extractive society excludes a part of the population since it no longer even offers them decent employment, and this part hovers around a half of the human race. This half whose lives have become precarious earn no more than the minimum wage, cannot obtain work that allows them to obtain professional qualifications or a minimum of stability that would enable them to plan for a life at a level above survival. Rubbish jobs for throw-away people.

Whereas industrial society promoted a rise in the social scale for at least three generations, extractive society consists of descending life stories: children have worse achievements than their parents or grandparents, and their life horizons have narrowed. The only known way of worsening the lives of half of society (from life expectancy to basic wellbeing as measured by stability and quality of relationships) is generalised violence.

To control this population that cannot be integrated, the model of accumulation through plunder has created a *police state* that is formally legal but dedicated to producing states of exception as a method of government to keep the 'dangerous classes' in order through a vast range of interventions running from corporate social responsibility – which allows for tax evasion – to discretional police or military intervention, focused on territorial control by force of arms in which the police force is charged with administering and managing things and bodies in an exclusive and excluding way (María Ferrero and Sergio Job, '*Ciudades made in Manhattan*', 2011).

Insofar as the model is an updating of the colonial break, we can see the different forms of oppression as they are lived out in the area of being and the area of non-being. They ways in which conflicts are settled in the two areas are different: in the first area there are areas for negotiation, the civil, labour and human rights of individuals are recognised, talk of freedom, autonomy and equality works, and conflicts are managed by non-violent means, or at least violence is the exception. In the area of non-being, which is also defined as the line below the human, conflicts are settled through violence and only exceptionally are non-violent methods used.[9] In areas where extractivism is supreme, where the humanity of people (first peoples, blacks and poorer people) is not recognised, they are subjected to what Walter Benjamin, in his essay 'Towards a Critique of Violence', called 'a permanent state of exception'. They cannot exercise the rights exercised by the white part or the middle class of society. The peoples of the favelas in Rio de Janeiro and São Paulo cannot peacefully exercise the right to demonstrate, because they are systematically attacked by the Military Police using bullets. The 'state of exception' is not a quirk of a bad government, but is determined by structural reasons, by a type of society in which one part of the inhabitants have no place, not as producers or even as consumers. In Agamben's words, present-day totalitarianism can be understood as 'the waging, through a state of exception, of a legal civil war that allows the physical elimination, not only of political adversaries, but also of whole categories of citizens who for what ever reason it is found impossible to integrate into the political system'.[10] We are facing one of the consequences of the crisis of the disciplinary society. What has happened is that the overflowing of the places of enclosure (prisons, hospitals, factories, schools, the family) has created the need for control in open areas, through marketing, indebtedness, consumption and pyscho-active drugs, the business in place of the factory, computerised systems instead of simple machines. But in the area of non-being these mechanisms do not work, among other reasons because heterogeneous relations predominate over hegemonic ones, and use values have more impact than exchange values. In a similar vein, Gilles Deleuze insists that 'human beings are not enclosed, but endebted', but warns that the mechanism of burdening people with debt does not work for two thirds of humanity, 'too poor to burden them with debt, too numerous to lock them up', and that the control society needs to create mechanisms to deal with 'the riots in the suburbs and the ghettoes'.[11] They have to be dealt with both by the state of exception and by imprisonment in the open, since for structural reasons they cannot be either integrated or indebted.

I believe that accumulation by plunder in the area of non-being should be given a different name, because it directly affects the lives of millions of indigenous, black and mixed-race people, landless rural people, poor women, the unemployed, informal workers and children in the outskirts

Accumulation Through Robbery and Systemic Violence

of cities. They are all suffering what the Zapatistas defined as the Fourth World War. As in all wars, the aim is to conquer territories, destroy enemies and administer the conquered areas by subordinating them to capital:

> The Fourth World War is destroying humanity insofar as globalisation is a universalisation of the market, and everything human that opposes the logic of the market is an enemy and has to be destroyed. In this sense we are all the enemy to be defeated: indigenous, non-indigenous, human rights observers, teachers, intellectuals, artists.
> (Sub-Comandante Marcos, 1999).

What is new about this new war is that the enemy is not the armies of other states, nor even other states, but one's own population, in particular that part of humanity that lives in the area of non-being. In short, get rid of the surplus people, turn territories into deserts and then reconnect them to the world market. The methods of eliminating peoples are not necessary physical death, though that is slowly spreading through the expansion of chronic malnutrition and old and new diseases, such as the cancer that affects the millions exposed to the chemicals used in monocultures and in mining.

When we call the current system a war against the poor or against those below, some facts begin to fall into place. Here I find some similarities between Segato's analyses and those of the Zapatista movement, in particular when they deal with the structural changes in the system, in which violence has ceased to be episodic: 'Crime and the accumulation of capital by illegal means has ceased to be exceptional; it has become structural and gives structure to politics and the economy.'[12] The accumulation of capital as it really takes place in present-day society is criminal, it threatens people's lives. This new modality of capitalism has transformed everything, including wars, which tend to be permanent. 'Their goal is not peace;' they turn into 'a form of existence' and, for the hegemonic power, are 'their ultimate form and dominion' (Segato, p. 57). In her characterisation of this type of war the author uses the terms 'plunder' and 'predatory and lucrative war', since the concept of conventional war between nation states as took place throughout the 20th century is no longer appropriate.

Segato includes among the forms or modalities of this new type of wars organised crime and paramilitary groups and para-states, which engage in informal wars. This is the context of the femicides, which are not hate crimes but power crimes. So Segato maintains that women's bodies are 'the corridor in which the structure of war is revealed (Segato, p.61). She insists that it is not an act of violence against an enemy warrior, but against fragile bodies in which 'the truculent threat aimed at the whole community' is made visible.

To sum up: an economy turned into a mafia system, one of plunder, as part of an eternal informal war to keep the powerful in power takes fragile bodies (women, but also girls and boys, first peoples and Afros) as military targets to warn society that the only way left is submission or death. Segato formulated the concept of masculine rule in Buenaventura, a port on Colombia's Pacific coast, when black women asked her what could be done to end the war and violence. 'Dismantle masculine rule,' was her reply. In a neoliberal regime where precariousness is everywhere (not only as regards work but in all areas of life) the male cannot fulfil this function and reacts violently against women and children.

That is why she regards these as power crimes. In this war for the control of lives and territories, the body 'is the ultimate form of control' in a system that has moved from discipline over bodies to absolute control over them.[13]

Democracy or concentration camp

The question I want to address is 'What political regime in Latin America corresponds to accumulation by plunder and the fourth war against the peoples?' My view is that militarisation is not the cause but a symptom of what is happening in the world and in every country. The reasons for police and military control of our societies have their roots in the efforts of big capital to perpetuate its power, in a period in which this domination was called in question, in particular since the world revolution of 1968.[14] To answer the question about the political system, I think we need to transport ourselves to present-day urban settings, the La Maré favela in Rio de Janeiro, the Northwestern commune in Medellín, the southern delegations of Mexico City like Iztapalapa, or any outlying community of one of the big cities of Latin America.

A brief overview tell us that these are areas in which everything is precarious: precarious neighbourhoods, houses and services for people

Accumulation Through Robbery and Systemic Violence

who live insecure lives, unstable and sometimes ephemeral. The streets are irregular and rutted, rubbish piles up on the pavements, there are almost no large civic buildings, but the Protestant churches are prominent, spacious, well-lit and with loud music. On the street corners you can see small groups of young people keeping watch and keeping control of the street. Depending on the area, they will be linked with the drugs trade or the para-state militias.

Total surveillance is set up, meticulous but at the same time diffuse. Who comes into and who goes out of the territory, what they do and how. Business and transport have to pay a tax to the drugs trade or the militias to be able to work 'in safety', to park your car without risking theft or damage, for any sort of economic activity you have to be checked by a nebulous 'them', who don't threaten directly but are omnipresent because their members live in the territory they control. If someone is noisy very late at a family party, the lads will knock on their door as a warning. Permanent observation, a watchtower with a view into every space.

What could we call this sort of territory? It is a concentration camp without barbed wire or physical watchtowers, though there are virtual watchtowers. 'It is a portion of the territory that is situated outside the normal legal order, but even so it is not just an exterior space.'[15] The camp is the material embodiment of the state of exception, the most important fact of modernity, where those who have no place in the system are confined: poor women and children, first peoples and blacks, poor people from town and country.

The camp as we know it today is the offspring of neoliberalism, accumulation by plunder or the fourth world war. It is a territory where 'anyone can kill you without committing murder',[16] because you belong to one of the throw-away categories. One phrase sums up this form of domination of bodies and life: 'The concentration camp and not the city is today the bio-political paradigm of the West.'[17]

Put differently, the camp is the form of domination that corresponds to the territories of the area of non-being under the fourth world war. Democracy does not exist. It is an electoral system to choose who is going to run the camp, but the fact of the camp can never be called in question because it is the structure of the form of domination. The concentration camp is the complement to extractivism, since confines within it those who – by their place in the geography of plunder – are obstacles to capital.

The state armed units have a fluid relationship with the paramilitary militias and the drugs trade.

Going against a certain common sense, exacerbated by the media, which talk about 'failed states' or the infiltration of crime into the state machinery, Segato emphasises 'the capture of the criminal camp by the state, the institutionalisation of criminality'.[18] Field studies have confirmed her insight. The journalist Oswaldo Zavala maintains that the Mexican political system exerts a control over organised crime, which has become subordinate to its control. The political system 'completely subdued organised crime, limiting the places where it can operate to specific cities, fixing its trafficking routes and, even more important, excluding it from political, civil, and military power' (*Los cárteles no existen*, p. 20). At the same time researcher Dawn Paley points out the existence of a thread linking capital accumulation and organised crime. She maintains that the war on drugs is an attempt to solve the long-term problems of capitalism, braking open territories previously closed to global capitalism (*Drug War Capitalism*). This war against peoples and populations seeks to displace communities to acquire the common resources the communities are trying to protect from destruction.

This analysis shows that movements for emancipation cannot go back to using institutions to support their cause, even if they will allow them to occupy them and neutralise their anti-popular and *mafioso* inclinations. Analysis and debate about structural violence in the current world system should provide food for thought for movements that want to transcend this world of constant violence and oppression.

Translated by Francis McDonagh

Bibliography

Agamben, Giorgio (2003) *Homo sacer. Sovereign Power and Bare Life*, Stanford, CA: Stanford University Press, 1998.

Agamben, Giorgio (2004) *State of Exception*, Chicago, IL, and London: Chicago University press, 2004.

Bebbington, Anthony (2007) *Minería, movimientos sociales y respuestas campesinas*, Lima, IEP.

Colectivo Voces de Alerta (2011) *15 Mitos y Realidades de la minería transnacional en Argentina*, Buenos Aires, Voces de Alerta.

Deleuze, Gilles (1996) *Conversaciones, Valencia, Pre-Textos*; English ed. *Negotiations 1972-1990*, New York: Columbia University Press, 1995.

Fanon, Frantz (1967, 2004) *The Wretched of the Earth*, Harmondsworth, 1967, and New York, 2004.

Ferrero, María y Job, Sergio (2011) "Ciudades made in Manhattan", en Núñez, Ana y Ciuffolini, María (comp.) *Política y territorialidad en tres ciudades argentinas*, Bueno Aires, El Colectivo.

Giarraca, Norma y Hadad, Gisele (2009) 'Disputas manifiestas y latentes en la Rioja minera', en Svampa, Maristella y Antonelli, Mirta ed. *Minería transnacional, narrativas del desarrollo y resistencias sociales*, Buenos Aires, Biblos, pp. 229-278.

Grosfoguel, Ramón (2012) 'El concepto de «racismo» en Michel Foucault y Frantz Fanon: ¿teorizar desde la zona del ser o desde la zona del no-ser?', *Tabula Rasa*, Bogotá - Colombia, No.16: 79-102.

Paley, Dawn (2018) *Drug War Capitalism*, Oakland, CA, 2014.

Segato, Rita (2016) *La guerra contra las mujeres*, Madrid, Traficantes de Sueños.

Subcomandante Insurgente Marcos (1999) '¿Cuáles son las características fundamentales de la IV Guerra Mundial?', 20 de enero en http://palabra.ezln.org.mx/comunicados/2003/2003_02_b.htm [Accessed 20/01/20].

Zavala, Oswaldo (2018) *Los cárteles no existen*, México, Malpaso.

Zibechi, Raúl (2016) 'El extractivismo es una guerra contra los pueblo', *Hora 25*, N° 122, La Paz, December, pp. 12-14.

Zibechi, Raúl (2017) *Descolonizar el pensamiento crítico y las rebeldías*, Lima, PDTG.

Zibechi, Raúl (2018) *Los desbordes desde abajo. 1968 en América Latina*, México, Bajo Tierra.

Notes
1. David Harvey, *A Brief History of Neoliberalism*, Oxford and New York, 1st ed., 2005.
2. Frantz Fanon, *The Wretched of the Earth*, Harmondsworth, 1967, and New York, 2004.
3. Raúl Zibechi, 'El extractivismo es una guerra contra los pueblos', *Hora 25*, no 122, (December 2016), 12-14.
4. Colectivo Voces de Alerta, *15 Mitos y Realidades de la minería transnacional en Argentina*, Buenos Aires, 2011.
5. Colectivo Voces de Alerta, *15 Mitos y Realidades de la minería transnacional en*

Argentina, p.15.
6. Norma Giarraca and Gisele Hadad, 'Disputas manifiestas y latentes en la Rioja minera', en Maristella Svampa and Mirta Antonelli, (ed.) *Minería transnacional, narrativas del desarrollo y resistencias sociales*, Buenos Aires, 2009, pp 229-278.
7. Giorgio Agamben, *State of Exception*, Chicago, IL, and London 2004.
8. Anthony Bebbington, *Minería, movimientos sociales y respuestas campesinas*, Lima, 2007.
9. Ramón Grosfoguel, 'El concepto de "racismo" en Michel Foucault y Frantz Fanon: ¿teorizar desde la zona del ser o desde la zona del no-ser?', *Tabula Rasa*, No.16 (2012), 79-102.
10. Giorgio Agamben, *State of Exception*, quotation translated from the Argentine edition, p. 25.
11. Gilles Deleuze, *Conversaciones*, Valencia, 1996, p. 284.
12. Rita Segato, *La guerra contra las mujeres*, Madrid, 2016, p. 76.
13. Segato, *La guerra contra las mujeres*.
14. Raúl Zibechi, *Los desbordes desde abajo. 1968 en América Latina*, Mexico City, 2018.
15. Giorgio Agamben, *Homo sacer. El poder soberano y la nuda vida*, Valencia, 2003, p. 216.
16. Giorgio Agamben, *Homo sacer*, p. 233.
17. Agamben, p. 230.
18. Segato, *La guerra contra las mujeres*, p. 216.

Transitions, Acts of Resistance and the Women's Movement: A View from Colombia

GINA MARCELA ÁRIAS RODRÍGUEZ AND LUIS ADOLFO MARTÍNEZ HERRERA

The current situation of transition in Colombia has been marked by considerable tensions: between cessation and continuation of violence, between the promises of the Peace Agreement and failure to comply with it, between the longing for peace and the obstacles to it. In this context civil society mobilisation, especially the experiences of the feminist and women's movements, have been important. They have resisted despite difficulties, insist and persist in securing the implementation of the Agreement and in finding methods of advocacy to build a less violent country.

I A Transitional Context: a decalogue of promises in unstable settings

The experiences of transition from dictatorships to democracies and from armed conflicts to peace – such as Central America, South Africa and, currently, Colombia – present scenes of contrasting feelings, in which the promise of overcoming the violence, the longing for negotiated solutions to the armed conflicts and the expectations for the end of often historic cycles of violence lead to a blurring of those feelings when it comes to implementation at local and regional level, which results in a deep gulf between the transitional longing and the specific actions in the territories, which fall far short of the public promises.

This gap between the promises of the transition and realities in the territories is made worse by a further contradiction: the peace agreements – the framework that normally structures the context of the transitions – set out the main lines officially agreed to resolve states of war or historic violence, but do not map out the actions that will make it possible to undo the results of violence that have been incorporated into structures of thought and feeling, or those imprinted on the bodies of those who have suffered violence and many forms of exclusion.

It is important to point out that transitional contexts that have framed periods of change mark the movement from critical conditions to the construction of *ideal* contexts (democratic models or societies that have socially recognised mechanisms for non-violent resolution of conflicts) Both appeal to the notion of historical memory, understood as a deposit of meaning in dispute, an incomplete mechanism and a political culture in transformation.

This knot tying together the *transitional context* and *historical memories* reveals a situation that places under tension the construction of historical narratives on which the foundations of social pacts can be built and this situation begins to erode the very foundations of the transition mechanism and its possibilities in everyday life during the armed conflict or the endemic acts of violence that it is hoped to end.[1]

II Putting the Colombian situation in context in the light of experiences of transition

At the beginning of the 1990s the French academic Daniel Pécaut offered an explanation of the violent conditions experienced in Colombia, stressing a paradox that made the Colombian situation somewhat different from others. On the one hand, he recognised a tradition of civic culture, relative economic growth, a monopoly of power by traditional parties and a sense of general stability, but at the same time he identified the existence of endemic violence, such as the rapid degeneration of the Colombian armed conflict, and defined the problem as follows: 'the complementarity of the functioning of the political system and intense, but diffuse, conflict'.[2]

So, while in the middle of the 20th century Latin America experienced many dictatorships, Colombia was free of them and experienced forms of government that operated under the cloak of democracy. But, precisely in the period of these governments that were non-military, but expressions of the traditional (Liberal and Conservative) parties, from the beginning of the 1970s to the beginning of the 21st century, Colombia held the world record for murders.[3]

Isn't this situation an affront to the rule of law? Doesn't it call into question the political structures that allow this situation to occur and to continue? Aren't these situations of (various sorts of) violence a historical situation that will destabilise the Colombian state in the Latin American context? In geopolitical terms doesn't it make us a destabilising state in a regional setting that is already in upheaval?

When the internal armed conflict had already lasted more than 50 years, at the end of the 1980s and the beginning of the 1990s the Colombian state initiated a second transitional process, and built a peace agreement with the guerrillas of M-19, Quintín Lame and the Popular Liberation Army (EPL) designed to end the endemic violence endured by Colombian society in the 1980s.

After this process of negotiation by the Colombian state with the guerrilla structures, a new period of violence began, starting at the beginning of the 1990s and ending in the middle of the first decade of the 21st century.

The general belief in social harmony and reconciliation was replaced by the greatest toll of victims since the beginning of the armed conflict. The most serious phase of the Colombian armed conflict, according to Ávila,[4] was recorded in the period between 1995 and 2005, when 60% of the victims of the 55 years of armed conflict were recorded, the highest number of clashes between guerrillas, military and the paramilitaries, the most significant war strategies in Colombian history were initiated.

It is possible to identify a third transitional context in the peace agreement signed between the government of Juan Manuel Santos and the FARC-EP, which proposed a global peace agreement, meaning that, in the words of the negotiators, that 'Nothing is agreed until everything is agreed.' There was to be no partial implementation of advances made at the negotiating table during the process; these would not be officially incorporated until the final signature by the two sides.

The negotiations had five thematic and one methodological point, which made up the objectives to be negotiated between the parties. The negotiations were carried out in commissions and sub-commissions, with negotiators for each of the topics. The topics were: *A Comprehensive Rural Development Policy*, one of the FARC's historic demands since its formation; *Political Participation*, involving an analysis of the conditions for the left's participation in politics in Colombia and the systems of community participation on which the FARC could have an influence; *Ending the Conflict*, under which there was an analysis of the real implications of the war in Colombia and the strategy for ending the war; *Solution to the Problem of Illegal Drugs*, under which the proposals of the two sides for ending the drugs trade were presented, since both sides regarded the drugs trade as the force behind violence in Colombia; and *Defining who are the Victims of the Armed Conflict*, a theme seen as a strategy for recognising the excesses of the war and incorporating the views of the victims and winning their support for ending the conflict. In addition to these points there was a discussion on a *Mechanism for Obtaining Endorsement of the Agreements*, which sought to establish the legal and political means of legitimating the agreements within the framework of the Colombian state.

Different international bodies have identified significant advances in the implementation process, particularly in central areas such as political participation, the end of hostilities, with the surrender of weapons by the FARC and the integration into civilian life of around 13,000 guerrillas, and advances in the establishment and start of activities in the transitional structures, such as the Commission for the Establishment of the Truth, Social Harmony, Non-Repetition and the Special Peace Courts. The main challenges continue to be in the territories in which different economic and political groups continue to pursue social practices based on power and authority and translated into illegal activities that continue to reproduce violent practices in the regions.

Currently 21 groups have been identified as 'dissident FARC groups', a minority: it is estimated that there around 3,000 women and men in these groups. But if we include the 135 members of these groups murdered since the signature of the peace agreement (26 November 2016),[5] together with the incomplete implementation of key areas such as land or guarantees for the political opposition, the situation is more delicate.

III The women's social movement and movements of resistance movements to war

In view of the complex panorama described above, women have raised their voices to say that war reproduces and intensifies practices of domination that are customary in and legitimated by the patriarchal system, in which women's bodies are taken over, thrown away and treated as objects as a mechanism to instil fear into communities and exercise territorial control, above all to 'wound the enemy's honour' and break down community ties. Women have raised their voices to denounce the fact that one of the deepest expressions of patriarchy is militarism, in which the most aggressive values and behaviour are taken to an extreme to devalue and humiliate the enemy by the use of women's bodies, encouraging contempt for life and difference and destroying territories without a second thought. This hyper-masculinisation and this way of practising violence on bodies – regarded by Rita Segato as a commandment of masculinity[6] – shows a need for supremacy in various dimensions – sexual, physical, political, economic, moral and military – which sustains any form of male violence and domination and treats women's bodies without mercy.

But women too have come up with initiatives to allow them to survive and resist: their ability to mobilise has allowed them to endure pain and also to have an influence in local and national arenas to make their voices heard, their rights recognised and make their longing to live in a peaceful country a possibility.

Women's initiatives were not the only ones that emerged in the 1990s, a decade that saw the creation of various initiatives for peace in Colombia, and among them the Women's Peace Route. The historian Mauricio Archila says that the 1980s was when the seeds were sown that produced the explosion of movements against war and in favour of peace.[7] Studies have shown that 'As the conflict escalated, great social efforts were being undertaken to transform the situation of our country.[8]

The Women's Peace Route began in 1996, when around 2,000 women converged on a town in Urabá in the department of Antioquia. Its motivation was to stand with and surround the women who were victims of sexual harassment by the armed actors. We took our inspiration from the experience of the Women in Black, a movement of feminist, pacifist and anti-militarist women who dressed in black to express their mourning and grief and to protest against the war and the occupation of Palestinian territories by Israel. In this way the Women's Peace Route took as its key principles, feminism, anti-militarism and pacifism, and organised visits to the regions that had suffered most from the armed conflict in order to be an expression of sisterhood and give publicity to the impact of the armed conflict on the lives and bodies of women and to demand that the Colombian state find a political, negotiated solution to the conflict.

Mauricio Archila argues that the women's movements were spurred to action, and even to take a leading role, by violence, not only motivated by traditional roles but also by a different attitude to war. This leadership was reflected in the powerful influence of the women's movement and LGBTIQ organisations in the negotiations in Havana, where they secured the establishment of a Gender Sub-Commission, considered by international experts as a historic achievement in processes of negotiation on armed conflicts around the world.[9]

The experience of resistance and persistence in the Peaceful Route found a powerful force in symbolism, ritual and spirituality to accompany women and to stimulate processes of political and emotional support for women,[10] and to lobby in the immediate surroundings about the need to build peace on the ground through non-violent resolution of conflicts, recognition of otherness, justice, autonomy and freedom.

With our slogan *We did not bear children for war*, we are saying that the power of motherhood and to give birth to children cannot be used to feed the armies of the illegal armed groups or the forces of the state. We claim for ourselves the right to live in peace, and for children and young people the right to a decent life with opportunities, leaving behind the structural violence that makes it easy for them to be recruited by armed organisations. In this connection it is worth noting that one of the reasons for the forced displacement of women is the fear that their children will be recruited in this way. A study carried out by UNICEF notes that between November 1999 and January 2013 the Colombian family welfare agency (ICBF) dealt with 5,252 children and adolescents of both sexes who had been freed from illegal armed groups.[11]

Furthermore, with our slogan *My body is not a war trophy* we want to draw attention to and publicise the forms of sexual violence on female bodies. *The Route* published an investigation entitled 'The Truth of Women Victims of the Armed Conflict' showing that 12% of the thousand women who gave evidence suffered sexual violence. The National Centre for Historical Memory records 15,738 victims of this crime, and this does not allow for under-reporting or the fact that the crime goes unpunished in 95% of cases.[12] Thus, just as patriarchy seizes women's bodies to exert violence, women's protest is also based on recognition of our own rights and the empowerment of the female body. This why the bared stomachs of women on pickets and marches carry the slogan *My body, first territory of peace*, making a demand for respect for bodies, territories and the right to a life free from violence in public and private.

At the same time the women's organisations, in particular the Peaceful Route, have developed special forms of organisation and connection, inspired by community experiences, everyday relationships, where we value every step we take locally, even privately, that is reflected in the decisions every woman takes if she takes part in workshops, meetings and demonstrations, often having to stand her ground when her own family members oppose these processes. In this sense, as Rita Segato says, women's politics is an everyday matter, in our closest ties; the emotional and affective dimension becomes a potent force for small transformations. In Segato's words, 'What we have to recover is their style of doing politics in these intimate spaces, where there is close bodily contact and things are less formal, but you can be cornered and abandoned when the rule of the public sphere is imposed.'[13] These everyday routines, the bonds, the spirituality, have enabled us to resist the imposition of violence and persist and insist – even in the midst of adversity – on the construction of a country in peace.

But we do not want just any peace. We did not organise and cross the country just to demand that the guns should fall silent; as well as this we imagined a future, a present and a future with social guarantees, in which ways of giving people a decent life can be offered. We worked for a positive peace.[14] In this sense we reaffirm our values in the slogan *Not a war to destroy us or a peace to oppress us*.

IV By way of conclusion

The transitional mechanisms under construction in Colombia are a necessary response to an armed conflict that lasted over 50 years, and need to be defended against the attempts of the current government to decry and dismantle what has been achieved so far.

Despite this position, some of the thinking behind the actions of the process need to be questioned if we are to move towards a negotiated solution of our conflicts. The scaffolding supporting the transition has not secured the wide consensus that would allow it to represent Colombian society's commitment to peace. Its institutional structures have not built local and regional links that would make it possible to turn the page on half a century of armed conflict.

The war thinking written into everyday life in the regions, especially into the lives and bodies of women, still operates as the biggest obstacle to the desires for peace, integration and national reconciliation. Added to this the agreements still not honoured by the Colombian state as compared with the agreements on paper, the interests of political and economic actors operating in the shadows and the increasing activities of illegal actors who have created illegal markets in the regions,15 show us a scenario in which talk of peace is losing its ability to inspire and, instead, increases frustration with agreements not kept.

Translated by Francis McDonagh

Bibliography

Aranguren, Juan Pablo. *La gestión del testimonio y la administración de las víctimas: el escenario transicional en Colombia durante la ley de justicia y paz*. Editorial Siglo del hombre, 2012.

Archila, Mauricio. *Idas y venidas. Vueltas y revueltas. Protestas sociales en Colombia 1958-1990*. ICANH, CINEP, Bogotá, 2003.

Árias-Rodríguez, Gina. '¿Mujeres víctimas? Víctimas empoderadas, dolidas y emputadas' en Asociación Colombiana de Facultades de Psicología. *Reconstrucción de subjetividades e identidades en contextos de guerra y posguerra*. Universidad de Manizales & Universidad Católica de Pereira, 201; ÁVILA, Ariel. *Detrás de la guerra en Colombia*. Editorial Planeta Colombia, 2019.

Galtung, Johan. *Human rights in another key*. Cambridge: Polity Press, 1994.

González, Katherine. 'Iniciativas de paz en Colombia'. *Civilizar* 10 (enero-junio de 2010), 35-54.

Instituto Colombiano De Bienestar Familiar, Organización Internacional Para Las Migraciones & Fondo De Las Naciones Unidas Para La Infancia. *Impacto del conflicto armado en el estado psicosocial de niños, niñas y adolescentes* (Convenio NAJ-661, Bogotá, noviembre de 2014). URL: en: https://repository.oim.org.co/handle/20.500.11788/541?locale-attribute=en

Martínez, Luis Adolfo. 'Retos del posacuerdo: Violencia homicida y prácticas sociales violentas en la ciudad de Pereira', en *Sociedad y Economía* 33 (2017) 289-310: https://dx.doi.org/10.25100/sye.v0i33.5633

Martínez, Luis Adolfo. (2017). 'Contrabando, narcomenudeo y explotación sexual en Pereira, Colombia', *Revista mexicana de sociología*, 79 (2017), 459-486. URL: http://www.scielo.org.mx/scielo.php?script=sci_arttext&pid=S0188-25032017000300459&lng=es&tlng=pt.

Onu-Mujeres. *100 medidas que incorporan la perspectiva de género en el Acuerdo de Paz entre el gobierno de Colombia y las FARC-EP para terminar el conflicto y construir una paz estable y duradera*, 2017.

Segato, Rita. *La guerra contra las mujeres*. Traficante de sueños, 2016.

Notes

1. Juan Pablo Aranguren, *La gestión del testimonio y la administración de las víctimas: el escenario transicional en Colombia durante la ley de justicia y paz*, Bogotá, 2012.
2. Daniel Pécaut, 'Colombia: violencia y democracia', *Análisis Político*, [S.l.], No 13 (May 1991), p. 16; ISSN 0121-4705. Available at : https://revistas.unal.edu.co/index.php/anpol/article/view/74721 [Accessed 14/01/20]
3. Luis Adolfo Martínez, 'Retos del posacuerdo: Violencia homicida y prácticas sociales violentas en la ciudad de Pereira', *Sociedad y Economía* 33 (2017), 289-310. http://sociedadyeconomia.univalle.edu.co/index.php/sociedad_y_economia/%20article%20/view%20/5633 [Accessed 16/01/20]
4. Ariel Ávila, *Detrás de la guerra en Colombia*, Bogotá, 2019.
5. This figure was published by the FARC party, which representation in both houses of the Colombian Congress under the terms of the peace agreement signed with the government of Juan Manuel Santos.
6. See the interview with Rita Laura Segato: https://www.lahaine.org/mundo.php/segato-por-que-la-masculinidad [Accessed 16/01/20].
7. Mauricio Archila, *Idas y venidas. Vueltas y revueltas. Protestas sociales en Colombia 1958-1990*, Bogotá, 2003.
8. Katherine González, 'Iniciativas de paz en Colombia', *Civilizar* 10 (Jan-June 2010), 39.
9. ONU-Mujeres, *100 medidas que incorporan la perspectiva de género en el Acuerdo de Paz entre el gobierno de Colombia y las FARC-EP para terminar el conflicto y construir una paz estable y duradera*, 2017. Relevant material is also available on the website of UN Women: https://www.unwomen.org/en/search-results?keywords=Colombia&country=d6ee99ec117b4a4e96bddd2aa800b086 [Accessed 15/01/20].
10. Gina Árias-Rodríguez. '¿Mujeres víctimas? Víctimas empoderadas, dolidas y emputadas', Asociación Colombiana de Facultades de Psicología, *Reconstrucción de subjetividades e identidades en contextos de guerra y posguerra*, Manizales, 2019: http://ridum.umanizales.edu.co:8080/xmlui/bitstream/handle/6789/3507/Reconstruccion_de_subjetividades_e_identidades_en_contextos_de_guerra_y_posguerra.pdf?sequence=1&isAllowed=y [Accessed 16/01/20]

11. INSTITUTO COLOMBIANO DE BIENESTAR FAMILIAR, ORGANIZACIÓN INTERNACIONAL PARA LAS MIGRACIONES & FONDO DE LAS NACIONES UNIDAS PARA LA INFANCIA. *Impacto del conflicto armado en el estado psicosocial de niños, niñas y adolescentes* (Convenio NAJ-661, Bogotá, noviembre de 2014): en: https://repository.oim.org.co/handle/20.500.11788/541?locale-attribute=en [Accessed 16/01/20]
12. http://www.centrodememoriahistorica.gov.co/micrositios/informeGeneral/estadisticas.html [Accessed 16/01/20]
13. Rita Segato, *La guerra contra las mujeres. Traficante de sueños*, 2016, p. 27.
14. Johan Galtung, *Human rights in another key*, Cambridge, 1994.
15. Luis Adolfo Martínez, (2017). 'Contrabando, narcomenudeo y explotación sexual en Pereira, Colombia', Revista mexicana de sociología 79 (3), 2017, 459-486: http://www.scielo.org.mx/scielo.php?script=sci_arttext&pid=S0188-25032017000300459&lng=es&tlng=pt. [Accessed 16/01/20]; Daniel Pécaut. 'Colombia: violencia y democracia', en *Análisis Político* No 13, (May 1991), 35-50: https://revistas.unal.edu.co/index.php/anpol/article/view/74721> [Accessed 16/01/20].

Part Two: Resistance

Care for the Common Home

GUSTAVO ESTEVA FIGUEROA

In this article I criticise the view that governments and international agencies have the responsibility for delivering global remedies for ecological problems, and describe initiatives and campaigns at ground level that are currently working throughout the world to care for the common home on a scale that is possible and appropriate.

I Introduction

How can you look after a house that is on fire? What should you do with the people who keep setting it on fire? Where do you start, and who with?

The planet is burning, not just the Amazon region. 'Climate change' or 'global warming' are just euphemisms. This is a climate collapse. The climate we used to have no longer exists and we know little about the one that is emerging. And in addition it is a climate tragedy. One's heart sinks at the thought of what has been lost for ever, the number of species and landscapes that have disappeared.

How can we look after our house when it continues to fall to pieces around us? Everyday there are condemnations of corporations and governments, of bodies identified as responsible. But we are all responsible: our way of life is destroying the common home. The scale of the task is enough to paralyse us, but it is also generating an immense variety of initiatives and actions. It is impossible to classify them: they are happening all over the world, on every scale, at every level. In this article I shall try to single out and compare two contrasting styles of action that illustrate in very different ways what it means to be concerned about the common home.

II The Greta style

There is no doubt of the talent, bravery and decisiveness of Greta Thunberg. With her simple and direct message she was able to drive millions of people to be concerned with our common home.

Greta focuses on the authorities. From the very start she pushed upwards: she called on the Swedish parliament to join the Paris accord. She broadened her focus, but kept the same direction. This position is intelligible because she accepted the hypotheses of the Paris accord and its main premise, that governments can and must fix the present crisis.

Millions of people share this attitude. It is useful to remember how it was formed. The movements sparked by the 1972 Club of Rome report broadened public awareness about the situation. The environmentalists put pressure on governments and institutions and prepared for a great battle in 1992, when the Earth Summit took place in Rio de Janeiro.

The huge publicity surrounding the United Nations Conference on Environment and Development was one of the reasons for organising it: it would broaden and deepen awareness of the earth's ecological problems. In fact it deepened confusion and uncertainty. When Rio calmed down and the 120 heads of state, the over 8,000 official delegates and a mass of ecologists, journalists and tourists all went home, it became clear that the conference had done no more than endorse the dominant ecological mythology.

The pessimistic forecasts made before the summit were fulfilled. Rio was to be the stage for a clever fraud. Ecology, which had called for the voices of change and social struggle, was to stay in the hands of 'the great and the good', who would have new consumer products to sell, now with green wrapping. The planet was to be placed in the hands of its enemies. The summit would not be about saving the earth, but about protecting created interests.

'Once we'd reached the summit, the only way was down.' This brilliant image of Juan José Consejo neatly sums up the perspective of ecologism after the Earth Summit.[1] The slogan that had united those who were trying to change the directions of society to more sensible life-styles was now powering an engine that did not belong to them. The summit made it clear that many policies and actions carried out in the name of ecology were moving in the opposite direction to the one they espoused. The radical critique of industrial society that initially inspired the 'greens' throughout the world was gradually coopted by the dominant establishments. In Rio it became its own negation, in yet another device to maintain the directionless rush of an industrialism destructive of nature and culture. The most clearly frustrating result was the globalisation of ecology.

The emphasis on 'global problems' such as the greenhouse effect, the destruction of the ozone layer or the disappearance of the rainforests revived the mechanistic myth of the governance or management of nature, on a global scale, using the new metaphor of the earth as a 'cybernetic totality'. Ever since, this emphasis has required 'global solutions' that would have to come from politicians, business leaders and technical experts with the ability to imagine and implement them.

This is the context, the mentality of global ecology and global remedies to be applied by those in control, in which Greta Thunberg entered the stage.

III Learning from experience

Nothing has been learned in government circles. The gospel of 30 years ago is still being preached. COP25 in Madrid in 2019 turned out to be a pale re-run of the 1992 Earth Summit. Representatives of 196 governments recognised the ineffectiveness of their prescriptions and agreements. Emissions of greenhouse gases, for example, which are still being presented as the enemy to be overcome, will reached their highest level in 2019. There has been no reduction at all, despite universal agreements and compromises – repeated again in Madrid.

A world administering the ecological crisis was the response from governments to the environmentalist movements in 1992. No-one has ventured to describe the task at all clearly, but the catechism it has produced is still being preached to the four winds. It guides policies and programmes, though it ignores the roots of our current problems. Instead of a radical critique of an industrial society that is patriarchal, capitalist, statist and anthropocentric that has permeated public awareness since the 1970s, a gospel has been proclaimed that is trying to rescue it from its contradictions.

Just as in 1992 the 'salvation of the planet' was entrusted to its chief agents of destruction, there is now an appeal to the reckless spirit of modern humans, to their blind faith in technology and their vocation to obedience. The doctrine of efficiency is supposed to be sustaining the endeavour: if we all save energy, make good use of resources and combat waste, guided and controlled by our authorities, we shall be able to have our cake and eat it: to continue the headlong dash of the industrial mode of production without destroying the earth. At ground level, on the other hand, people have been learning. Since 1992 the deafness coming from above had undermined confidence in governments and institutions. Even in Rio voices very different from the official ones were to be heard, often as mere whispers in corridors. They talked about more local, more feminine ecologies. They insisted in following their own inspiration, based on their rich and diverse cultures, instead of following the illusion of the common future preached by the ecocrats and their planetary government. They broke radically with the universal slogans, especially those associated with development. They showed that ecological problems are not merely technological or moral issues, and that they threatened the very achievements of modern civilisation.

The grassroots groups resisted the pretensions of globalisation, determined to face down the new missionaries who, in the name of the salvation of the earth, were continuing to threaten lands and cultures. They called for ecological problems to be localised, identifying the spaces in which they originate and can be corrected. They showed that all that can be done on a planetary scale is to destroy the planet. They showed that global thinking is in fact impossible. We have to think small. Only local action can succeed in changing course.[2]

Since then ground level has advanced towards a radical rediscovery of our own soil, of the spaces and perspectives of each group. A new hope was nurtured and new avenues of thinking were mapped out.

IV The current insurrection

On 6 December 2019, at the Madrid climate summit, young people and indigenous spoke out and gave vent to their frustration and anger. They were no longer prepared to go on listening to empty promises. They will go on protesting in the streets 'until instead of hearing us they start listening to us for once'.[3] But they are already in another place.

The anti-system movements that began with the 1994 Zapatista rising have formed new waves of popular demonstrations in the 21st century. They coherently expressed the diversity of the discontents with the dominant system, particularly with representative democracy. 'Let them all clear off!' said the Argentines in 2001. Ten years later the *Indignados* in Spain announced firmly, 'My dreams won't fit in your ballot boxes!', while the Greeks warned that they would not abandon the squares they were occupying until 'all of them' went away. Occupy Wall Street, in New York, insisted forcefully: 'You have demands when you think that governments can meet them; that's why we don't.' Since October 2018 the 'yellow vests' in France have been radically rejecting all systems of representation. In 2019 the demonstrations in Lebanon and Haiti have been trying to break with all the 'political classes'. All over the world, especially in Latin America, rebellion is spreading. 'We shall install a parallel government,' said the Mapuche leader Aucán Huilcamán in Santiago de Chile.[4] José Ángel Quintero, an Añu indigenous leader, observed from Venezuela: 'The rebellion we are proposing starts with the need to win back our own hearts, which is nothing other than recovering our ability to think and feel with the earth.'[5] At the same time a radical critique of the dominant system was in circulation. It had been shown that capitalism had reached its internal limit, and could no longer reproduce itself. It was clear that the modern nation state, the political form of capitalism, had run out of steam. What was also very clear was the oligarchic character of so-called representative democracy.[6] Counter-summits have taken on another meaning in this century.

They continue to act as a critical mirror to the actions of governments and international agencies, but they are also means of organisation. Extinction Rebellion activists, for example, present in many settings, don't stop at protest. Convinced of the failure of conventional approaches and of the uselessness of voting, lobbying and organising petitions, they have turned to a strategy of 'disruptive, non-violent civil disobedience – a rebellion'.[7] Greta Thunberg came to Madrid. With other young people she led the March for the Climate. This symbolised a twofold commitment: without abandoning pressure on the authorities, they called for direct action. Demands alone strengthen the system that produces the destruction. We cannot care for our common home while this system lasts.[8]

3.1 Anti-patriarchal sense
The main root of the evil we face is to be found in patriarchy, already treated as normal in modern society. Dismantling it implies, first and foremost, abandoning the hierarchical system that defines it and its

compulsion to replace all life-forms with artificial creations. The proposals on this topic of the Zapatistas and the Kurds in Rojava are well-known, but there have been many more. For example, the Planetary Movement for the Pachamama, launched in Germany in 2010, is trying explicitly to protect Mother Earth and care for life. Many other initiatives, such as Vikalp Sangam in India and Crianza Mutua in Mexico, place care for life at the centre of social organisation and insist on eliminating all hierarchy and any system of authority, control and subordination, dismantling the dominant oligarchic structures from the base. A radical shift has been taking place in the political perspective of the social struggle. As demonstrated brilliantly by Yásnaya Aguilar, a Mixe woman, at an event organised by the Zapatistas in April 2018, the aim now is not to fight against 'a Mexico without us' (without the first peoples), but 'us without Mexico'. It is not separatism; it is not an attempt to create another nation state as patriarchal as the present ones. The 'feminisation of politics', which Yásnaya also represents, has nothing to do with the division of quotas between women and men. It is a different way of running social and political affairs, not based on hierarchical principles, and one that re-establishes care for life at the centre.[9] The anti-patriarchy thrust also implies abandoning the route of development in favour of many other ways of promoting good ways of living and breaking with the economic mentality, encouraging instead concepts like community and autonomy.[10]

3.2 A sense of proportion

Economic fluctuations have long since stopped being economic cycles and have become size cycles. The scale of economic activities places them beyond the possibility of human control. Nonetheless, as a response to every crisis the institutions increase the scale of control, aggravating the problems they are claiming to solve. Instead of centralisation and unification, what is needed is to 'cantonise' economic activity.[11]

A mouse the size of an elephant would collapse, for lack of proportion. The same would happen to an elephant the size of a mouse. Proportionality is a feature of both natural and social entities. At the base of society people know this through experience and common sense. Instead of constructing mechanisms and organisations on a national and international scale, they concern themselves with what is within their reach. They make collective and communal agreements that recover the sense of limits and proportionality. They know from experience that they cannot trust in national and international structures. They adopt an alternative perspective.

Localisation means going beyond localism and globalisation. Initiatives are localised, but not closed in their contexts. They are open to similar units to unite and produce coalitions and alliances for shared learning, defence, solidarity and to build political links, without adopting national, international or global perspectives to guide their activity. They use their connections strategically to deal with their continuous conflicts with corporations or the state. As the initiatives interact and combine, they have to construct stable forms of harmonic interaction on various scales. For this purpose they use options that avoid bureaucratic and centralised power structures. The Mexican National Indigenous Congress, for example, which connects thousands of scattered communities from different peoples and cultures, has adopted the principle: 'We are an assembly when we are together; we are a network when we are apart.' The Congress has been in operation for 25 years, without a central office, leaders or bureaucratic structures. The point is to reduce the necessity for coordination at national or international level. People can coordinate in all their activities, without subordination or control, eliminating the need for something or someone to coordinate. Collective endeavours beyond the local scale do not need to define in advance a political body or to adopt a specific doctrine or design. Bridges are built when the time comes to cross them.

In May 2019 the formation of the Global Tapestry of Alternatives was announced. This is an attempt to identify and link initiatives that challenge the dominant system on a local, regional and national scale, encouraging shared learning, solidarity and political links. It seeks to contribute to the formation of a critical mass of initiatives to reconstruct collective life on new principles.[13]

From 6 to 11 September 2019 activists from a wide range of countries met in Iceland to compare political strategies of grassroots groups in order to defend each other collectively and interact harmonically and convivially across local, regional and national spaces. They discussed democratic confederalism, libertarian municipalism, communalism and other political tools that retain a horizontal approach and democratic elements constructed at the social base.[14] The Global Tapestry of Alternatives and the Iceland meeting illustrate current efforts to find ways of linking people's initiatives, without constructing bureaucratic or representative structures and avoiding doctrinaire dogmas or utopian promised lands.

3.3 Common sense
Common sense is usually associated with sensible and realistic ideas that don't need any rational filter to be accepted. Common sense is what we have in a community. It flows from rules shared by a group that generally are not written down and are the product of experience accumulated throughout the history of the particular group. Common sense, in almost all groups, includes concern for the wellbeing of their members and care for the common home. The patterns of behaviour dominant in present-day societies are in open contradiction with the common sense of most people. An increasing number of people have realised that patterns of thinking and behaviour that have come to seem normal are destructive and operate against their interests, their wellbeing and their surroundings. The current proliferation of initiatives and movements frequently refer to getting back to common sense.

3.4 Autonomous subsistence
The movement to get back to and revive commons (everything to do with community) is now completely general. It is overturning the process of enclosures that created the dominant system and continues its battle against autonomous subsistence.

There are numerous examples all over the world. The most notable example is perhaps Via Campesina (established in 1993), the largest popular organisation in human history. The organisation has a presence in all international public forums concerned with food and tries to influence public policies at national and international levels. Its main activity, however, is on the land. The rural people that make it up are day by day putting their redefinition of food sovereignty into practice: to decide for ourselves what we will eat and to produce it. At present, small farmers, mainly women, feed 70% of the world's population, whereas agribusiness, which controls over half the world's food resources, feeds only 30%.[15]

3.5. Reviving the soil and virtue
More and more people are becoming convinced that it is only in specific local areas that the critical virtue that is lacking under present conditions.

In 1992, very far from the Earth Summit, in a small German village,

Ivan Illich and his friends were talking about how this new civic virtue was being shaped, which was concerned with 'the form, order and direction with which we act, informed by tradition, tied to the place and validated by the elections carried out within our customary range of action'. These were 'the practices recognised as good within a shared local culture that gives priority to the memories of a place'. These enable people to resist the new ecocracy, 'the ecological experts who preach respect for science but foment contempt for historical tradition, local knowledge and self-limiting earthly virtue'. This Hebenhausen declaration on soil can still be regarded today as a fascinating marker of what happens at the base of society.[16]

V The open breach
Ordinary people who every day express their freedom and physical integrity 'sustain the human condition in the midst of the utmost precariousness, united in service to others and in the absolute desire for a more human world. They have started to produce a change... In this way the earth is becoming pregnant with their commitment.'[17]

Translated by Francis McDonagh

Bibliography
Aguilar, Yásnaya. 'Nunca más nosotrxs sin ustedes! ¡Un nosotrxs sin Estados!', *Pueblos en camino* (11 December 2019): https://pueblosencamino.org/?p=5886

Berry, Wendell. 'Out of your Car, Off your Horse', *Atlantic Monthly* (February 1991), 61-63.

Esteva, Gustavo. *New Political Horizons*, forthcoming.

EDUCA, '25 años de Cumbres del Clima, sin resultados: Jóvenes e indígenas expresan su hartazgo', 6 December 2019, https://www.educaoaxaca.org/25-anos-de-cumbres-del-clima-sin-resultados-jovenes-e-indigenas-expresan-su-hartazgo/

Extinction Rebellion https://rebellion.earth

Groeneveld, Sigmar *et al.* 'La Declaración de Hebenhausen sobre el suelo' en *Opciones* 3 (1992); http://davidtinapple.com/illich/1990_

declaraion_soil.PDF

Illich, Ivan. *The Wisdom of Leopold Kohr*, 1994: https://centerforneweconomics.org/publications/the-wisdom-of-leopold-kohr/

Kohr, Leopold (1992) 'Size Cycles', *Fourth World Review* 54 (1992).

Mooney, Pat. *Who will feed us? The Peasant Food Web v. The Industrial Food Chain*, ETC, 3rd ed. 2017: https://www.etcgroup.org/sites/www.etcgroup.org/files/files/etc-whowillfeedus-english-webshare.pdf

Quintero, José Ángel. *El último despojo después de la tormenta. Cambio climático, desaparición de la casa y extinción de la territorialidad añuu. Cuatro advertencias y un camino*. México: Ediciones Unitierra, 2019, p.17.

Rodríguez, Arsenio. 'Breve encuentro con Ernesto Sábato. Una reflexión sobre el destino del mundo' *Wall Street International* en español (31 October 2019) https://wsimag.com/es/cultura/58503-breve-encuentro-con-ernesto-sabato [9 diciembre 2019].

The Ecologist. *El nuevo ecologismo. Manifiesto de los ámbitos de comunidad*. México: Editorial Posada.

Trujillo, Juan. 'Chile: la revolución mapuche', Red Latina Sin Fronteras, *Desinformémonos* (24 November 2019). URL: https://desinformemonos.org/la-sublevacion-mapuche-en-chile/ [11 December 2019]

Notes

1. Quoted in Gustavo Esteva, Preface to *The ecologist. El nuevo ecologismo. Manifiesto de los ámbitos de comunidad*, Mexico City, 1995, p. 9.
2. Wendell Berry, 'Out of your Car, Off your Horse', *Atlantic Monthly* (February 1991), 61-63.
3. EDUCA, '25 años de Cumbres del Clima, sin resultados: Jóvenes e indígenas expresan su hartazgo', 6 December 2019, https://www.educaoaxaca.org/25-anos-de-cumbres-del-clima-sin-resultados-jovenes-e-indigenas-expresan-su-hartazgo
4. Juan Trujillo, 'Chile: la revolución mapuche', Red Latina Sin Fronteras, *Desinformémonos* (24 November 2019): https://desinformemonos.org/la-sublevacion-mapuche-en-chile
5. José Ángel Quintero, *El último despojo después de la tormenta. Cambio climático, desaparición de la casa y extinción de la territorialidad añuu. Cuatro advertencias y un camino*, Mexico City, 2019, p.17.
6. See Gustavo Esteva, *New Political Horizons*, forthcoming.
7. Extinction Rebellion UK: https://rebellion.earth; International https://rebellion.global/ (both accessed 15/01/20).
8. Greta realised that appealing only to the authorities was futile. She showed this by the way she spoke to them in New York: 'How dare you – you have stolen my dreams and my childhood' *The Guardian*, 23 September 2019: https://www.theguardian.com/environment/video/2019/sep/23/greta-thunberg-to-world-leaders-how-dare-you-you-have-stolen-my-dreams-and-my-childhood-video . In Madrid she was even harsher: 'The leaders are

betraying us and we will not let this go on', *Europa Press*, 6 December 2019: https://www.europapress.es/sociedad/medio-ambiente-00647/noticia-greta-thunberg-lideres-nos-estan-traicionando-no-vamos-dejar-eso-siga-sucediendo-20191206210428.html

9. Yásnaya Aguilar,'Nunca más nosotrxs sin ustedes! ¡Un nosotrxs sin Estados!', *Pueblos en camino*, 11 December 2019: https://pueblosencamino.org/?p=5886 [11 diciembre 2019).

10. For further development of these themes, see Gustavo Esteva, *New Political Horizons*.

11. Leopold Kohr, 'Size Cycles', *Fourth World Review* 54 (1992), 10-11; Ivan Illich, *The Wisdom of Leopold Kohr*, 1994: https://centerforneweconomics.org/publications/the-wisdom-of-leopold-kohr/ [Accessed15/01/20].

12. www.globaltapestryofalternatives.org [Accessed 15/01/20].

13. https://democraticconfederalism.earth/contact-us/ [Accessed 15/01/20].

14. Pat Mooney, *Who will feed us? The Peasant Food Web v. The Industrial Food Chain*, ETC, 3rd ed. 2017: https://www.etcgroup.org/sites/www.etcgroup.org/files/files/etc-whowillfeedus-english-webshare.pdf [Accessed 15/01/20].

15. Sigmar Groeneveld, et al. 'La Declaración de Hebenhausen sobre el suelo', *Opciones* 3 (1992), 16.

16. Ernesto Sábato, in: Arsenio Rodríguez, 'Breve encuentro con Ernesto Sábato. Una reflexión sobre el destino del mundo',*Wall Street International* en español, 31 October 2019: https://wsimag.com/es/cultura/58503-breve-encuentro-con-ernesto-sabato {Accessed 15/01/20].

Women in Their Various Struggles: Spiritual Activism as 'Other' Knowledge

SUSAN ABRAHAM

This essay is a reflection on the Roundtable on Women's Resistances at the Resist! conference. It argues for building coalitions and solidarities with women around the world, even as patriarchal violence, racism, sexism, classism and other forms of discrimination reflect contextual variances. While postcolonial feminisms argue for transnational feminist communities by dissolving geopolitical borders, South American feminists argue that the border is exactly where the most capacious imagination of life occurs. The difference between the two approaches, however, are less significant in light of their shared commitments to the wellbeing of women, children, the poor, and life on the planet.

For a while now, feminist theory in Western and Northern Euro-America has been struggling with the impasse accorded by postmodern feminism. The *Resist!* Conference held on May 27-30, 2019 in Mexico City provided ample evidence for such an assertion. Postmodern feminism, a staple of academic feminism in Northern Euro-America emphasizes culture, discourse and language. It is a very productive engagement, resulting in keen analyses of the ways in which power, knowledge, subjectivity and language intertwine to create matrices of oppression. Here, advocacy for a dissolution of borders for the sake of political work challenges transnational feminism to conceive of resistance as beyond borders. On the one hand, transnational feminism asks women to join forces with each other despite their cultural, racial and nationality differences.

On the other hand, particularly for the women of South America, routinely written out of such analyses, the issue of context and the material reality of bodies feeding Western and Northern Empire is the basis of resistance and the creation of identity. Borders also take on a materiality that have political significance. Drawing on contemporary Chicana scholars' work on Gloria Anzaldúa's "spiritual activism," and in conversation with postcolonial feminist thought, this essay argues that women's knowledges, in order to become effective at resisting Empire, necessarily requires Anzaldúan relationality of intra-becoming, by recognizing that borders exist. Postcolonial feminist thought conversely, argues that all geo-political identities are the creation of Euro-American colonialism and sustained to create fractures and splits in any form of alliance. Yet, these two perspectives may not be as distinct as one may grasp on a first reading. Teasing out the strands of possible alliance between these two feminist approaches is a goal of this essay.

The roundtable that I participated in was entitled "Patriarchal State and Systemic Violence." The participants were indigenous activists and community leaders who provided testimony on the many violences faced by women in their contexts. Such a panel was in stark contrast to the many academic conference panels that I otherwise regularly participate in, here in North America. As an "unconference," that is, a mode of thinking and being with people who do not identify immediately as "academics," *Resist!* resisted coercive forms of exclusion by imperial systems of recognizing knowledge. Academics have a way of hanging out with each other, to the exclusion of activists and field workers. We were asked to think about the following questions: What is patriarchy and how does it manifest itself; what is the "Patriarchal State;" what are the characteristics of patriarchal violence; what are the subjectivities that participate in patriarchal violence; how do people resist patriarchy and why are some religious fundamentalisms use gender ideology to discredit movements against patriarchy? In exploring these questions, a number of oppositional sites became evident. One is what is recognized by many as "identity politics." Another is the split between individual agency/wellbeing/health and survival often opposed to collective agency, health and survival of the many. Another is the academic split between so-called academic knowledge and "non-academic" knowledge. The roundtable dealt with these oppositions by pointing out how these functioned to keep colonial rationalities and power in place.

Susan Abraham

The roundtable made clear that the ways in which traditional conferences privilege particular forms of knowledge is a form of violence through exclusion. Even panels that are constituted to challenge the status quo function with such violence. The presumed "political expertise" of academics writes out, elides and erases forms of activist and engaged political work that many women with no access to institutional academic structures. In fact, the astonishing fact is that women from other than Euro-America continue to be written out of even feminist knowledge. Audre Lorde, in a poem written in 1989 wrote:

The US and the USSR are the most
powerful countries
in the world
but only 1/8 of the world's population.
of that, ¼ is Nigerian,
½ of the world's population is Asian.
½ of that is Chinese.
There are 22 nations in the middle east.
Most people in the world are Yellow, Black, Brown, Poor, Female, Non-Christian
and do not speak English.
By the year 2000 the 20 largest cities in the world will have one thing in common
None of them will be in Europe none in the United States.[1]

And of course, most of the world is excluded from Euro-American academies because they do not mirror the concerns, methodologies and knowledges of the empire. Their entry into these academies are hampered by economic, political and neocolonial policies aimed at sustaining capitalism in the West and grinding poverty elsewhere. Postcolonial feminist scholars have attempted to address such exclusion in various ways. For example, a critical intervention in postcolonial studies by Chandra Talpade Mohanty argued for feminism without borders, in order to decolonize theory and practice solidarity. However, Mohanty's work, is an example of discursive feminist politics as its focus is the discursive space in which knowledge about "third world women,"[2] circulate. As she emphatically asserts:

Women in Their Various Struggles: Spiritual Activism as 'Other' Knowledge

The relationship between "Woman" (a cultural and ideological composite other constructed through diverse representational discourses—scientific, literary, juridical, linguistic, cinematic, etc.) and "women," (real, material subjects of their collective histories) is one of the central questions the practice of feminist scholarship seeks to address. This connection between women as historical subjects and the representation of Woman produced by hegemonic discourses is not a relation of direct identity or a relation of correspondence or simple implication. It is an arbitrary relation set up by particular cultures.[3]

Institutional power structures, of church, nation, society and academy circumscribe the lives of Third World women. In making her argument for borderlessness, Mohanty points to the "internationalization of economies and labour forces."[4] Transnational corporations seek both extractive opportunities in the third world, while also seeking cheap labor to transform extractive raw materials into goods for consumption. These economic policies have redrawn the boundaries of the nation-state in such a way that it is "no longer an appropriate socioeconomic unit for analysis." In fact, the term "third world" itself has become meaningless, since "systemic socioeconomic and ideological processes position the peoples of Africa, Asia, Latin America and the Middle East, as well as minority populations (people of color) in the United States and Europe" in a third-world like relationship to the state, *within* these states. Borderless political work is critical if gains are to be made for women in contexts marked by racism, sexist violence, colonialism, imperialism and monopoly capital.

Third-world subjects are particularly impacted by racist citizenship and immigration laws. In her prescient analysis of this idea, Mohanty argues that citizenship and immigration laws are fundamentally about creating insiders and outsiders. In a manner unlike the earlier colonial context, contemporary neoliberal capitalist states "operate through unmarked discourses of citizenship and individual rights."[5] She identifies a feature of neoliberal violence that is so subtle in its effects, that it remains invisible. As she argues, in colonial contexts it was easy to note the sharp sexual division of labour in which white masculinity and white adventure led to masculine conquest. In contemporary contexts in contrast, an impersonal but highly masculinized bureaucracy organized around themes of rationality, calculation and orderliness once again consolidates patriarchal and masculinist power. Even as such hegemonic masculinity attracts the analytic criticism of Western feminists, missing is the almost invisible creation of the highly racialized interactions of rationality, calculation and orderliness, in which white feminism is implicated. Racism is the ideology that both creates the system of exclusion from which people of color are excluded from the recognized rationalities, calculation and orderliness of the state, and also, the system by which excluded people are automatically judged to be outsiders or "minorities."

For transnational feminists, how to do feminism without racism continues to be an enormous challenge. Mohanty's chapter entitled 'The Politics of Experience,' in her book *Feminism Without Borders*, provides a cogent roadmap.[6] Feminists, in emphasizing the category of 'experience,' often falsely universalize women's experience. There is no 'universal' women's oppression, for example. Women's oppressions are specific to their historic and cultural locations. Here, more than domestic forms of patriarchy, recurring themes of internationalized economic and cultural forms of exclusion lead to solidarities and collectivities of resistance. Instead of "experience," often taken to be immediately accessible, understood and named, Mohanty offers another view. Experience for example, cannot be named outside of the frameworks that we use to represent it. Further, "experience" often has the valued position of a psychologized, internal and individualized knowledge that does not need verification. For Mohanty, such appeals to experience do not lead to the overturning of systems of oppression. She writes:

> Since experience has a fundamentally psychological status, questions of history and collectivity are formulated on the level of attitude and intention. In effect, the sociality of collective struggles is understood in terms of something like individual group relations, relations that are commonsensically seen as detached from history. If the assumption of the sameness of experience is what ties woman (individual) to women (group), regardless of class, race, nation, and sexualities, the notion of experience is anchored firmly in the notion of the individual self, a determined and specifiable constituent of European modernity. However, this notion of the individual needs to be self-consciously historicized if as feminists we wish to go beyond the limited bourgeois

ideology of individualism, especially as we attempt to understand what cross-cultural sisterhood might be made to mean.[7]

Another issue that inhibits the creation of transnational feminism is an overemphasis on locality. This may seem to be a contradictory idea, especially when Mohanty's emphasis is otherwise on historicized and localized struggles. But Mohanty's delicate point is that an overemphasis on any particular struggle has the same effect as the overemphasis on the category of experience. Instead, what is important is to focus on the "temporality of struggle," a focus on time, that is a direct challenge to the idea of temporal "linearity, development and progress that are the hallmarks of European modernity."[8] The focus on time, which suggests an "insistent, simultaneous, nonsynchronous process characterized by multiple locations, rather than a search for origins and endings" is a far better tactic for transnational feminist coalitions.

Mohanty's work represented an early constructive proposal for transnational feminists. Yet, as the *Resist!* conference also made clear, localized forms of resistance have lessons to teach. Chicana resistances for example, are not single-issue resistances. They respond simultaneously to multiple forms of violence, since oppressions intersect in myriad ways in the lives of South American women. What also became clear is that activists may be sidelining the role of spirituality, especially as it connects with activism. Such spiritual activism was a hallmark of Gloria Anzaldúa's work, especially in her groundbreaking book *Borderlands/La Frontera: The New Mestiza*. Anzaldúa has inspired a number of transnational thinkers to think beyond the binary of secular and religious, which is another way in which the Euro-American academy constrains transnational feminisms. In an essay detailing similar political insights, Sonya M. Alemán and Flor de Maria Olivo argue that the "Itzpapalotl Spirit" guides a form of resistance *writing* practice.[9] The authors write:

> In particular, we sought to decolonize and reclaim indigenous narratives of indigenous female warriors ...especially since Anzaldúa described writing as a form of activism and referred to herself as a "writer-warrior." Thus we discovered the goddess Itzpapalotl, a female warrior goddess and fertilizing force who served as a caretaker of productive and fruitful realms that generate life, learning and ingenuity....The Aztec

goddess Itzpapalotl, more commonly known as the Obsidian Butterfly, is described as the warrior leader or queen of the *tzitzimime*, or star goddesses, and rules a dominion known as Tamoanchan. A *tzitzimime* herself, she is depicted by a striking skull appearance and skeletal body with the wings of a silkmoth or butterfly. Given these features, she exists in duality, possibly as both spirit and flesh. Portrayed as a zombie-like figure with eagle talons for fingers and jaguar wrists, she interacts in past, present and future.[10]

The Itzpapalotl spirit provides for the authors a metaphysics of interconnectedness and complex temporality that decolonizes by challenging Euro-American modes of individualist agency and justice, all touchstones for the kind of Northern feminist political thought that erases the complex realities of violences faced by women from the global south. As a form of spirituality that is deliberately challenging to Euro-American theory, theology and spirituality, Itzpapalotl spirituality emphasizes the specificity of localization even as it calls for its transcendence. For example, Itzpapalotl is the "keeper of a creative, fruitful and transformational kingdom," in which she sustains life-giving knowledge-producing dynamism. Learnedness and existence are intimately related in this view. Writing then is a "site of radicalized knowledge production by Chicanas/os about their marginalization in order to dismantle that disenfranchisement and build solidarity among its readers."[11]

As a deliberately non-Christian space, Itzpapalotl spirituality is a particular form of Chicana driven activist spirituality. It helps, as Anzaldúa had argued, to displace Western thought. It invokes cultural memories of ancient knowledges and borderland epistemologies to challenge and dislodge the cultural hold of European colonial and North American neocolonial knowledges. These border knowledges however, function in a similar way to the engaged activism of thinkers like Chandra Talpade Mohanty. Whereas Mohanty had argued for transnational feminism without borders and geo-political identities, with the goal of creating spaces that challenge Euro-American hegemonic knowledge production for the political liberation of all women, Alemán and Olivio assert a strategic identity based knowledge than embraces indigenous women's forms of knowledge as knowledges that lead to survival. Mohanty, Alemán and Olivo all also draw on Anzaldúa in complex ways to counter patriarchal violence and to form communities of active resistance. Another critical idea that these authors share is that of a complex temporality. Complicating time also complicates the spaces we inhabit.

Indeed, such was Anzaldua's original contribution: spiritual activism was grounded in "her understanding of a metaphysical network of interconnections between all living things, rather than rooted in an organized religion's worship of a monotheistic god. Spiritual activism is a state of *conocimiento* that emerges after crisis, conflict, or tensions between the self and the world have triggered a shifting perspective to one that eschews socially constructed divisions based on identity politics; restructures the fractured mind, body and spirit; and catalyzes a desire to pursue social, economic and political justice for all."[12] Alemán and Olivio's view coincides perfectly with Mohanty's impetus to decolonize feminism. Mohanty asserts that the most important feminist work that needed to be done is the work of decolonizing feminism, because feminism under Western eyes simply reinscribed Western values of self and identity, creating the untenable framework of identity politics. Conversely, a politics of identity looks at how patriarchy, the patriarchal state, neocolonial globalized capitalism and Western colonialism create the conditions of fracturing alliances and coalitions because of identity politics.

Feminist solidarity then can draw on both models. In the case of an Anzaldúan form of spiritual activism, it can emphasize the work that has to be done with special attention to identity at the border. The border, precisely because it stands for so many exclusions and divisions becomes the site of resistances. It decolonizes by drawing on the wisdom of indigenous traditions, many of them predating the conquest of the Americas. It insists on the life-world of all creatures and beings, arguing for an interconnected spirituality of life and existence. In a different way, postcolonial feminism argues that feminists cannot be subservient to borders and identities and need to frame agency and resistance across the borders of nation and cultures. Its form of engaged activism does not focus on spirituality, but understands the interconnectedness of feminist resistance. It does so because it believes in the flourishing of women everywhere. Resistance then, in the immortal words of Anzaldúa is:

Susan Abraham

Una lucha de fronteras/A Struggle of Borders
Because I, a mestiza,
continually walk out of one culture
and into another,
because I am in all cultures at the same time,
alma entre dos mundos, tres, cuatro,
me zumba la cabeza con lo contradictorio.
Estoy norteada por todas las voces que me hablan
simultaneamente.[13]

Bibliography

Alemán, Sonya M. & Olivo, Flor de Maria. "Guided by the Itzpapalotl Spirit: Chicana Editors practice a form of Spiritual Activism," in *Frontiers: A journal of Women's Studies*, Volume 40, Number 1, 2019, pp. 245-271.

Anzaldúa, Gloria. *Borderlands/La Frontera: The New Mestiza*. San Francisco, CA: Aunt Lute, 1987.

Mohanty, Chandra Talpade. *Feminism Without Borders: Decolonizing Theory, Practicing Solidarity*. Durham and London: Duke University Press, 2003.

Notes

1. Excerpted from epigraph to "Cartographies of Struggle: Third World Women and the Politics of Feminism" in Chandra Talpade Mohanty, *Feminism Without Borders: Decolonizing Theory, Practicing Solidarity* (Durham and London: Duke University Press, 2003), 43. Anzaldúa was mostly correct in her assessment. A simple internet search on the 20 largest cities in the world as of 2018 reveals that New York city and Los Angeles are among the top twenty, while 14 of the largest cities in the world are in Asia alone. See https://www.archdaily.com/906605/the-20-largest-cities-in-the-world-of-2018.
2. While this nomenclature has fallen out of favor in Euro-American academic contexts, both Anzaldúa and Mohanty use it as a short-form for the material context in which the excluded woman is reproduced.
3. Chandra Talpade Mohanty, "Under Western Eyes: Feminist Scholarship and Colonial Discourses," in *Feminism Without Borders: Decolonizing Theory, Practicing Solidarity* (Durham and London: Duke University Press, 2003), 19.
4. Mohanty, "Cartographies of Struggle," in *Feminism Without Borders*, 44.
5. Mohanty, "Cartographies of Struggle, in *Feminism Without Borders*, 64.
6. Mohanty, "The Politics of Experience," in *Feminism Without Borders*, 106-123.
7. Mohanty, "The Politics of Experience," in *Feminism Without Borders*, 115.
8. Mohanty, "The Politics of Experience," in *Feminism Without Borders*, 120.

9. Sonya M. Alemán and Flor de María Olivo, "Guided by the Itzpapalotl Spirit: Chicana Editors practice a form of Spiritual Activism," *Frontiers: A Journal of Women's Studies*, Volume 40, Number 1, 2019, pp. 245-271.
10. Sonya M. Alemán and Flor de Maria Olivo, "Guided by the Itzpapalotl Spirit: Chicana Editors practice a form of Spiritual Activism" in *Frontiers: A Journal of Women's Studies*, Volume 40, Number 1, 2019, 263.
11. Ibid.
12. Sonya M. Alemán and Flor de Maria Olivo, "Guided by the Itzpapalotl Spirit: Chicana Editors practice a form of Spiritual Activism," *Frontiers: A Journal of Women's Studies*, Volume 40, Number 1, 2019, 253.
13. Gloria Anzaldúa, *Borderlands/La Frontera: The New Mestiza* (San Francisco, CA: Aunt Lute, 1987), 76.

Part Three: Spiritualities

Relational Wisdom and Spiritualities in Abya Yala

SOFÍA CHIPANA QUISPE

The text presents the interrelation of the ancestral wisdom and spiritualities of Abya Yala, which are intertwined with each other, forming a living fabric of reciprocal relationships that restore balance and harmony, based on the wisdom of nurturing life, which enables the repairing of the human uprooting of the link to and interaction with the Community of Life that enables the care and defense of Mother Earth.

I Living word

I start this sharing evoking the forces of the wise people of *Abya Yala*[1] to center the connection with the ancestors who accompany the search for wisdom from good understanding, good will and good work, which are created in the experience of relational spiritualities that seek the harmony of life in our territories. As it is profoundly expressed on the altar of life of the Mayan peoples from the *kajb'al*[2], the four orientations that interweave the integrality and the cyclical process of life, which walks together with the force of the rising sun of the east, lives its necessary transformations in the darkness of the night of the west, linking with the vital breath of all beings from the south, and directing the purposes of the paths in the direction of the north.

From the link with the strength that comes to us from the diverse beings that inhabit our territories, I offer these words that seek to interweave themselves with the various words that persistently contribute their colored threads to the Great Network of Life. We seek to continue restoring the balance and harmony so necessary in our times, in which the threat of the dominant power of human ambition stalks, violently, and kills. But it does not silence, as we can see in the various people that stand up and decide to walk: there are no bullets or military forces that stop them, because the fire of dignity is emerging from the connection with the old memories of resistance that remain recorded in our bodies.

Here, I leave these words to continue "corazonando"[3] (understanding through the heart).

II Ancestral wisdom in resistance

The long journey of the ancestral wisdom in Abya Yala went through times of ruptures and emptiness, which meant the alienation of identities and the loss of territories, founded in the attribution of cultural superiority based on the analogy between the sacred and religion, from which knowledge was sustained in medieval Europe. The transgression of sound doctrine when assuming plural knowledges was deemed heresy or witchcraft. So the attribution of power to a few "elect" who came to our territories, invalidated the knowledges and spiritualities linked to the cycles of the cosmos of the conquered peoples, from the hegemonic religious discourse that continues in our times.

Five centuries resisting

I recall some memories of the wise Andean, Luzmila Carpio, when she described her people happily without church. For, in our territories, religion undertook a great desecration of knowledge and wisdom intertwined with spiritualities, although for the missionary entourage of Christianity it was a campaign of extirpation of idolatries, as a war against the devil, as widely narrated in the various chronicles of doctrinal priests and encomendero[4] holders:

> According to a theory of the time, formulated by José de Acosta in his Natural and Moral History of the Indies (1590), after the total Christianization of Europe, the Devil moved to America: "But, finally, since idolatry was excised from the best and noblest part of the world, [the Devil] withdrew to the most remote, and reigned in this other part of the world, which although much inferior in nobility, in greatness and breadth it is not".[5]

In this way, not only were the sacred narrative of the peoples (symbols, stories, textures, art, spaces, times, experiences) invalidated, but also their knowledge and wisdom, to give way to the Christianization of the territory, in order to erase every vestige of the presence of the devil.

In that context, Luzmila's words are understood, since the Christian presence generated a series of ruptures that disharmonized life in our territories by stigmatizing them as demonic. For life was conceived in its entirety, having as its axis two profound principles, balance and harmony, from which one overcomes the dualistic notion of good and evil, the sacred and profane, from the criterion of reciprocity and complementarity which seeks to harmonize the forces that unbalance life.

What would we have been, if we could have been?
Despite the diverse affirmations to continue being, the great colonial burden expanded from the prevailing hegemonic system of "the west", under the name of civilization and now development. As people, we live under permanent siege in the process of our knowledge, languages, spiritualities, sciences and technologies, which were not considered to be such, because they are assumed to be primitive, depriving them of fully unfolding. In turn, the spaces of 'civilizational' knowledge that we access follow the colonial thread of the mental monoculture that silences our knowledge and other knowledge in connection with the cosmos, which is known only by walking it, looking at it, touching it, feeling it, loving it.

Although we carry a series of colonial coverings in our being and knowledge, we perceive the creative force of the millenary seeds sown by grandmothers and grandfathers. They are germinated, nourished by the wisdoms and spiritualities that maintained the courage of resistance of our beautiful pluriverse, expressed in seeds, colors, faces, languages, melodies, flavors, festivals, rituals, times, spaces, and territories, inhabited by the great diversity of the living.

We continue to make our way, despite the intimidation of patriarchal and racist capitalism, which, day by day, leaves us with the pain of the bodies that fall like seeds before time, because on the horizon we glimpse an opportune time to establish our pluri-nationalities from the territorial cushioning that blurs the logic of the borders of colonial nationalism, in order to continue raising life and to be raised by it.

III The wisdom of the loving upbringing of life

To present some interweaving of wisdom and ancestral knowledge, I evoke the living word of the Quechua, *kachkaniraqmi*, which translates as, "I remain," "I still continue being." This word is pronounced when a person wants to express that in spite of everything one still is, one still exists; in the same way many nationalities, people and communities in Abya Yala, live intertwining with each other to form a living fabric, based in the impulse of memory. The past is the source of the understanding of life, from which we are learning to reread and tell our stories and wisdom recreated over and over again, with the various broken, burned threads, but also with those that begin to spin.

Reciprocal wisdom in the upbringing of live

The walking words of the people connected to their ancestry have in common the demand for the care and defense of Mother Earth. It is not a recent demand, nor a 'popular environmentalism'. These are other ways of being that resisted death throughout 300 years of colonial violence and imposition, which also extends over the more than 200 years of the nation states based on the modern myth of unlimited development that related to the cosmos as matter and its inhabitants as objects that must submit and be mastered. Therefore, extraction policies are accompanied by the extermination of the populations that oppose this purpose, thus justifying the criminalization of resistance and the militarization of territories, because the other ways of existing and being pose a threat.

That other way of being in the cosmopraxis[6] of the people starts from the understanding of the relational ontology from which are assumed "other ways of relating more symmetrically between humans, animals, plants…"[7] Everything has life, its time and its place in the Cosmos, where humanity is part of the great community of interrelations that flow reciprocally and in a complementary way to raise life. This wisdom is expressed when the diversity of beings are equated with the category of people to establish a symmetrical and loving relationship:

> All who live in this pacha are persons; the stone, the earth, the plants, the fruits, the water, the hail, wind, diseases, sun, moon, the stars, we are all a family; to live together, we help each other, we are always in continuous conversation and harmony.[8]

Loving relationships are not an exclusive quality of people, but also of other beings:

> We tell the fox: you are going to advise us how the agricultural season will be. You don't have to eat the sheep either, because you have your big guinea pigs, that's what you are going to be eating and that's how nobody is going to bother you.[9]

In this way it is possible to establish being raised by other beings, from the sensibility of knowing at what time and how the animal-person, the seed-person, the river-person are conversing...

Likewise, relationships with spirits, sources of life, guardianship forces, the ancestors, are not only given through rituals that seek to foster the harmony of the community, but also in the permanent communication of everyday work. Therefore, the wisdom of the upbringing of life has a two-dimensional meaning: it is empirical because it has to do with concrete relationships and it is spiritually symbolic because it palpitates with the vital forces of the Cosmos.

On the other hand, the wisdom of mutual upbringing seeks the existence of the greatest biodiversity that inhabits the various territories, since reciprocity seeks the interrelationship of all beings, since the absence or discomfort of one affects relationships in the community of the living.

In this way, the ethics of responsibility for the continuity of the cycles of the cosmos, in the reciprocal upbringing of life, guides Good Living as a cosmic-political proposal, which reflects the feeling that everything is interconnected, interrelated and is interdependent. This implies, according to the wise Maya xinca Lorena Cabna, the *Ixina*, "the awakening of cosmic consciousness to embrace a new era for bodies and territories".[10] The feeling is expressed by the 2,500 women from more than 130 villages in Brazil who engaged in their meeting saying: 'territory is our own life, our body, our spirit."[11]

We are at the right time to redirect our knowledge, based on our wisdom and relational spiritualities, so Fernando Huanacuni will pertinently say: "To return to our wisdom is not to go back, but to reconstitute ourselves in the principles and values that do not have time, that do not have space."[12]

IV The fabric of relational spiritualities in Abya Yala

The encounter with the millenary roots of our peoples is based on the dynamic force of our spiritualities that returns us to our constitution of relational beings, following the cosmic principle that everything has its time and place. From this principle, they are able to generate the necessary links, even with the imposed religion of Christianity, gradually assumed in a series of appropriations of some symbols interpreted from the cultural matrix itself, as can be seen in the experience of some peoples in a significant divergence with dogma and popular Catholicism.

Interweaving our spiritualities

The resurgence of the ancestral spiritualities of the underground, surpasses their comparison as popular religiosities linked to Christianity, as Sylvia Marcos rightly states:

> "Indigenous spirituality" is not a matter of church, personal devotion or individual beliefs. It is what unifies and identifies the collectivities; what gives them cohesion. It is what is recovered from the ancestors, which gives meaning to their political and social struggles. It is not, in short, an institutional religion.[12]

And Josef Estermann points out:

> It is not limited to a certain field or to certain institutions and specialists, but it is present in all aspects of life, from birth to death, from planting to harvest, and of course in everything that has to do with the bettering of the conditions of life.[14]

For his part Vicenta Mamani affirms, based on her experience that:

> Spirituality is part of cultural identity and vice versa, because there is no identity without spirituality, nor spirituality without identity. Therefore, we are convinced that spirituality springs from life.[15]

Although ancestral spiritualities are interwoven from relational ontologies, we perceive that they take the risk of staying within tradition in order to safeguard certain forms. On the other hand, the territorial uprooting of the populations that move towards the cities generates a series of influences that move them away from reciprocity in the upbringing of life, which results in the cutting of their roots.

In the interweaving of relational spiritualities, we cannot deny that some peoples have assumed Christian religious practices as part of their walk. However, in the processes of exchange, it will be necessary to consider that interculturality in our contexts, part of the intracultural process, which allows people to drink from their own wells.

The sources of relational spiritualities

But the influence of Christian dualist spirituality generated a series of hierarchical relationships that extended into the various spheres of life, thus placing men on a higher level, subordinating women. It cannot be denied that in that relationship there were also traces of an ancestral patriarchate, which is not comparable to the Western patriarchate that feminized even the male body of the "Indian." The "inferior" condition of women limited their relationship with the civilization space that allowed them to recreate their wisdom and spiritualities, as Vandana Shiva puts it:

> The women of the Third World, whose minds have not yet been stripped or colonized, are in a privileged position to make visible the invisible opposite categories of those who are guardians [...] Their voices are the voices of liberation and transformation that provide new categories of thought and new exploratory directions.[16]

They knew how to weave the life that resists death, as Vicenta Mamani asserts about her people: "the Aymara woman is the protagonist and contributes to identity and spirituality from community practices."[17] In turn, for Sylvia Marcos, "women are actively recapturing ancestral spiritualities to decolonize those religious universes they were historically forced to adopt".[18]

The strength that comes from women is not accidental, since it is a connection with the long memory of the people to restore the upbringing of life, surpassing the short memory of the more than 500 years in which male strength was accentuated. Thus, they manage to link to the vital female force named in various ways, because their recognition will help to overcome the imbalances, as Shiva puts it:

> The recovery of the feminine principle is a response to the multiple dominations and deprivations not only of women, but also of nature and non-western cultures. She defends the ecological recovery and the liberation of nature, the liberation of women and the liberation of men, who by dominating nature and women have sacrificed their own humanity.[19]

Women, in their connection with ancestral spiritualities and knowledge, are recognized as part of living peoples, whose life depends on the ability to recreate their identities from what is imposed, as they do with their clothing, to which they have given their own nuances, since while they are being transformed, they also create and transform themselves. It is not about simple techniques, but about offering life, as can be seen in the learning of textile work, where "[…] the textile operating chain does not consist only in a set of dry technical sequences. Young women must also learn to introduce life into textiles."[20]

In the processes of ties, ancestral spirituality regains the awareness that "all types of living beings depend on others for their existence and are intertwined in an immense fabric that evolves continuously",[21] which confronts relations "[…] based in human sexuality following heteronomous norms, [which] is reflected in the construction of sexual cosmic thinking".[22] By thus restoring the reciprocity of life in the cosmos, the binary notion of the feminine and masculine is overcome, since these are vital sources that flow in reciprocity in diverse beings and in diverse ways.

V Intentionalizing the reciprocity of healing

To conclude, I intertwine the words, aware that the disharmony caused by the imbalance in Mother Earth has to do with our sick humanity, since in the great network of relationships good living is not gestated when one member is not well.

The recent events that we witness in our territories, reflect the resistance of outraged human communities to the authoritarian power that sustains various oppressions on bodies, following the old colonial patterns that are sustained with the power of weapons and in the religious discourse that is imposed as absolute truth.

Together with the affective memory of the healers, we "intentionalize" the reciprocal force of healing as a historical project of encounters, shared cyclical rituals, spiritualities that dialogue to continue bringing up life and letting us grow up. Decolonizing our beings, knowledge, and power, we can interweave, from the plural wisdoms, the harmony of full life, because "healing myself, heals you and healing you, I heal myself, healing you and I heal Mother earth and all living communities."

Bibliography

Arnold, Denisse. "Hacia una antropología de la vida en los Andes", in Galarza, Heydi (ed). *El desarrollo y lo sagrado en los Andes*. La Paz: ISEAT, 2017, pp. 11-40.

Cabnal, Lorena. Documentos en construcción para aportar a las reflexiones continentales desde el feminismo comunitario al paradigma ancestral originario del "Sumak Kawasay", Buen Vivir. Association of Indigenous Women of Santa María Jalapa.

Marcos, Sylvia. *Mujeres, indígenas, rebeldes, zapatistas*. México, Eón, 2013.

Esterman, Josef. "El mercado religioso y la Religión del Mercado", in *ISEAT, Religión y desarrollo en los Andes*. La Paz: ISEAT, 2008.

Mamani Vicenta. *Identidad y espiritualidad de la mujer aymara*. La Paz: Misión de Basilea-Suiza y Fundación SHI-Holanda, 1999.

Shiva, Vandana. "Mujeres en la naturaleza: la naturaleza como el principio femenino Vandana" in Agra Romero, María Xosé (comp.). *Ecología y feminismo*, Granada, Ecorama, 1998.

Van den Berg, Hans. *La tierra no da así nomás: Los ritos agrícolas en la religión de los aymara-cristianos*. Cochabamba: Hisbol-UCB/ISET, 1990.

Notes

1. In the language of the Kuna people of Panama, it is translated as land in full maturity, an expression assumed by the various peoples as an alternative to the colonial name of Latin America.
2. Symbol of the integrality of life from the four cardinal points expressed in the Mayan altar.
3. An approach to the reflexive process where it is important to listen to the heart, which understanding moves through.

4. Translator's note: An encomendero was a parcel of land and all its resources [indigenous people included] granted to colonizers.
5. Van den Berg, Hans. *La tierra no da así nomás: Los ritos agrícolas en la religión de los aymara-cristianos*. Cochabamba: Hisbol-UCB/ISET, 1990, 195. [All quotations translated by this article's translator.]
6. It concerns the relational practices of co-participation in the world.
7. Arnold, Denisse. "Hacia una antropología de la vida en los Andes", in Galarza, Heydi (ed). *El desarrollo y lo sagrado en los Andes*. La Paz: ISEAT, 2017, pp. 11-40, here 16.
8. Apaza Ticona, Jorge. "Cosmovisión andina en la crianza de la papa", in van Kessel, Juan & Larrain, Horacio (Eds.). *Manos sabias para criar la vida, tecnología*. Quito: Hombre y Ambiente, 1997, 101-125, here 103.
9. Ibid., 106.
10. Lorena Cabnal, *Documentos en construcción para aportar a las reflexiones continentales desde el feminismo comunitario al paradigma ancestral originario del "Sumak Kawasay", Buen Vivir*. Association of indigenous women of Santa María Jalapa AMISMAXAJ, 15. URL: https://amismaxaj.files.wordpress.com/2012/09/buen-vivir-desde-el-feminismo-comunitario.pdf. [Accessed: 20 June 2017].
11. First Indigenous Women's March: "Territorio: nuestro cuerpo, nuestro espíritu", 16 August 2019. URL: http://apib.info/2019/08/16/primer-marcha-de-las-mujeres-indigenas-territorio-nuestro-cuerpo-nuestro-espiritu/?lang=es [Accessed: 20 September 2019].
12. Fernando Huanacuni. "El Buen Vivir, tradición indígena". *Agenda Latinoamericana*, 24-25. Here 24. URL: http://servicioskoinonia.org/agenda/archivo/obra.php?ncodigo=747 [20 September, 2019].
13. Sylvia Marcos. *Mujeres, indígenas, rebeldes, zapatistas*, México, Eón, 2013, 122.
14. Esterman, Josef. "El mercado religioso y la Religión del Mercado", in *ISEAT, Religión y desarrollo en los Andes*. La Paz: ISEAT, 2008, 59.
15. Mamani, Vicenta. *Identidad y espiritualidad de la mujer aymara*. La Paz: Misión de Basilea-Suiza y Fundación SHI-Holanda, 2000, 25.
16. Shiva, Vandana. "Mujeres en la naturaleza: la naturaleza como el principio femenino", 15 June 2014 in, Agra Romero, María Xosé (comp. and translator). *Ecología y feminismo*, Granada, Ecorama, 1998, 5. URL: https://www.slideshare.net/lgoren/vandana-shiva-la-naturaleza-como-el-principio-femenino [Accessed: 20 September 2019].
17. Mamani, Vicenta. *Identidad y espiritualidad de la mujer aymara*, 2000, 107.
18. Marcos, Sylvia. *Mujeres, indígenas, rebeldes, zapatistas*, 2002, 4.
19. Shiva, Vandana. *Mujeres en la naturaleza: la naturaleza como el principio femenino*, 2014, 8.
20. Arnold, *Hacia una antropología de la vida en los Andes*, 2017, 19.
21. Ibid.
22. Cabnal, Lorena. "Acercamiento a la construcción de la propuesta de pensamiento epistémico de las mujeres indígenas feministas comunitarias de Abya Yala" in *Feminista Siempre. Feminismos diversos: el feminismo comunitario*, España: ACSUR-Las Segovias, 10-25, here 13. URL: https://porunavidavisible.files.wordpress.com/2012/09/feminismos-comunitario-lorena-cabnal.pdf [Accessed: 20 June 2017].

Theology of the Quilombo: Afro-Brazilian Spiritual Resistance

CLEUSA CALDEIRA

Immersed in a structurally racist society, which tries to camouflage a necropolitical approach under the myth of racial democracy, Afro-Brazilian spiritual resistance has taken place through the subjectification process of becoming black. A paradoxical process: on the one hand, painful because of the racist violence that afflicts us physically and, on the other, joyous because we are building our identity as an Afro-Brazilian people. It is a process that implies the recovery of our imago Dei *(Image of God) and the emergence of a new humanity.*

I Introduction

The black population represents more than half of all Brazilians, close to 55%. They total some 110 million black women and men. There are 59.4 million black women in the population of Brazil, accounting for 51.8% of all Brazilian women. The period from 2003 to 2013 saw an increase of 54.2% in the murder of black women while in the same period there was a decline of 9.3% in the murder of white women. For every 200 homicides in Brazil, 75 of the victims are black.[1] These numbers throw a stark reality into relief that should be the cause of serious social unrest. Yet for many, this reality is seen as something normal, since the death of blacks has become nothing more than a historical process of naturalisation.

A consideration of Afro-Brazilian spiritual resistance implies a change vis a vis our African roots that is ethical, epistemological, political and spiritual. In order that this might be possible, we need to recognise the historical construction of racial classification as a fundamental element of the building and perpetuating of global capitalism, and which led to the ontological exclusion of blacks, relegating them to the status of sub-humanity.

To talk of Afro-Brazilian spiritual resistance is to reflect on the subjectification processes of becoming black, since racism, in addition to denying the humanity of black people, so legitimising their subjugation also produces their imprisonment in a false *imago*. Becoming black, would appear in the Brazilian context, to be the sole possibility for securing historical redemption, and, therefore, the theological place where the theology of the Quilombo can be addressed.[2]

II Racism as a process of (self)annihilation

To be black is to be condemned to "live in a space where you do not exist", where a human existence is denied to you, as Frantz Fanon reflected when thinking of the wounds inflicted by colonialism.[3] Following Fanon's approach, decolonial thinking makes it clear that the theoretical and historical make up of racism took place at the heart of the modern/colonial system as a core axis of the global power network that proved itself to be the most efficient and durable instrument of universal dominance.[4] Racism, nevertheless, is not only phenotypical and racial discrimination by individuals but above all a form of hierarchy of individuals exercising domination.

Achille Mbembe, calls this dominance "necropower" a popular recommendation for establishing a licence to kill, a necropolicy for the setting up of "cities", or rather zones deliberately marked out as areas where the freedom to commit murder is enshrined.[5] For Mbembe, necropolitics is linked to the survival of the colonial system in the present day, that is to say to the submission of life to the power of death.[6]

In the context of Brazil, this necropolicy has its own characteristics. These can be typified as genocide of the black population. Following the abolition of slavery, this genocide was pursued to make the population "whiter" through a process of interbreeding. The essence of this policy continued to be an ontological exclusion which held black people to be inferior to white. The Brazilian elite devised this policy with the intention of purifying the population to the point where the black element of the population became extinct.[7] This miscegenation, or interbreeding, far from being a natural outcome of races coming together, as many thought to be the case, was no more than a political project to make the population more white. It was carried out through the rape of black women, mulattos being the outcome, epitomising the mythical symbol of "racial democracy".

This myth of racial democracy, however, is nothing more than the perfect metaphor for *Brazilian* racism, in other words, camouflaging a policy of black annihilation; institutional racism that, "only confers one "privilege" to the blacks, that is to say the right to become white, both within and without.[8] Fanon had already warned that there was only one destiny for the black people: to become white.[9]

> To be black is to be constantly violated, continually and cruelly, with neither pause nor rest with two aims in mind: to ensure you embody the presence and ideas of the white Ego and to reject, deny and cancel the essence and presence of the black man.[10]

Neusa Santos Souza, the Afro-Brazilian psychoanalyst, has also focused consideration on the impact on the black population of both racism and the fixation on being white. It no longer is a matter of being a white person, as "whiteness" has now transcended the fact of just being white. It has become fetishised. According to Souza, this fetish leads to a desire for self-annihilation: "the black man, in his wish to become white, desires no more nor less than his own extinction. His ambition is, at a future point, no longer to exist; his hope is not to be or to have never been".[11] And this process of self-annihilation leads to the start of a kind of self-persecution in order to eliminate any negroid traces, being it by hair straightening, nasal plastic surgery; the denial of links with Africa, the breaking with black brothers and sisters of ties of affection, beliefs, politics or religion.

Fanon criticises this imprisonment of black people, attributing it to the whites' historical construct of the blacks that, "rejects present reality and duty in the name of a mythical past".[12] Without wishing to deny that the subjugation of the African peoples to the level of slavery had a devastating effect on how we think about them, this is why we talk about the absolute need to decolonise our subjective approach.[13] A first step in this process of decolonising subjectivity implies overcoming how we have regarded black people, that is to set aside colonialization and slavery as the only ontological reference points in the configuration of black subjectivity.[14] Obviously, this also entails taking on both the historicity and the necessary hard work to recreate oneself vis a vis others.

III Quilombism as radical decolonisation

Despite the bodily afflictions inherent in racist violence, the black population never let itself be entirely subjugated. It always found ways both to resist and to reinvent itself. This unique approach to become black within the context of Brazil is known as "Quilombism".[15] From the outset of colonialism in the 15th century, the quilombo appeared as a form of Afro-Brazilian resistance that was ethical, political, economic, cultural and spiritual. This refutes the idea that the black population were passive, accepting of their lower condition without any form of resistance.

Historically, throughout the three centuries of black slavery, the quilombo – in an institutional sense – represented a black centre operating a social system that was an alternative to the oppression of the colonial approach. Flight to the quilombo constituted a reaction to colonialism and, as such, a means of resistance.[16] There were quilombos that were so well set up and organised that they constituted a threat to the colonial system. Palmares is the best known and significant in Brazil. It was known as the Republic of Palmares and, as such, was held to be the first attempt to found a new Free State in the Americas.[17]

After the abolition of slavery, there was move for quilombos to change from being institutions to ideological constructs, becoming symbols of Afro-Brazilian resistance in the struggle for self-affirmation and understanding.[18] Ever since, the mystique of the quilombo has fed the dream of black freedom providing elements for building of a national historical awareness with, above all, a reaffirmation of the African heritage and the construction of an Afro-Brazilian identity.[19]

According to Abdias Nascimento, the quilombo works as a guiding thought, an energy that inspires models of dynamic and alternative organisations.[20] Always flexible in adapting to circumstance, the quilombo or 'quilombism" is constantly updating itself, reflecting the contextual demands of history and geography".[21] And there is more. The quilombo places a limit on the rhythm of colonial genocide, giving rise to the possibility of a new way living one's life. It is, thus, perfectly legitimate to think of quilombism in terms of racial decolonisation as conceived of by Fanon since a flight to the quilombo signalled the birth of someone as a political being through a refusal to accept a barbaric existence that both denied and forcibly removed one's humanity.

Decolonisation arises as a force of a refusal that is in opposition to an attachment to the practice of colonialization. The strength of this refusal marks the individual's first action as a political being. In fact, the *political protagonist* – or simply the Fanonian one – *comes to the world and to himself through this first act, which is the capacity to say no.*²²

The black person from the quilombo is the political black person and whosoever becomes this, who takes on the task of building their own identity, in so doing collectively and organisationally opposes all and any violence that degrades humanity.

IV "Becoming black, as an ontological experience"

"........people are born black, light brown, brown, maroon, reddish amongst other colours but *becoming black is a triumph*"
Lélia Gonzalez

The rebuilding of our Afro-Brazilian identity is both a hard task and a sweet victory. We talk about rebuilding because we are aware of the harms caused by epistemological and ontological racism on our own subjectivity and intersubjective relations. In considering this rebuilding, we need to deconstruct the false identities which have been conferred on us, as being black, light brown, brown and so on; identities of subjugation which signalled our inferiority and subordinate status. Becoming a black man or woman, represents no less than the difficult challenge of giving birth to the Afro-Brazilian identity. This cannot be considered as a pre-conceived identity. It is precisely from this metaphysical imprisonment that we blacks are struggling to escape. To be black is not a question of metaphysics. Rather, to be black is an ontological experience, a way of being. "To be black is to become black".²³ This affirmation in itself constitutes a revolutionary step given that black people were denied any ontological attributes and were therefore deprived of any political or legislative legitimacy.

The decolonisation of our subjectivity is interwoven with the acceptance of our historicity, which is to say that we become our own masters and develop our own ways of being. It is to engender a process that implodes the racist structures of Brazilian society that placed black people at their basest level. It is to be no longer invisible, to become the protagonist and developer of our own identities and historical memories. Becoming black in a context where our humanity has been denied is to develop alternative approaches to communities, to create new groupings of black people, to value our ancestry, culture and African values. It is, effectively, the experience of sharing in an act of redemption that implies the complete humanisation of everyone.

V Spiritual resistance: Muquifu and the Igreja das Santas Pretas

The museums of Muquifu[24] and the Igreja das Santas Pretas (the Church of Black Saints) constitute one of the more original and significant instances of spiritual resistance in contemporary Brazil. Both evidence the recognition of the human dignity of the black shantytown populations. Both Mquifu and the Igreja das Santas Pretas are authentic quilombos that arose from the acts of subjectivation of those black men and women who opposed the socio-historical determination that had relegated them to subhuman status. What is more, these quilombos imposed a limitation on the necropolitics which did not recognise their territory as sacred.

The Muquifu – Museum of Quilombos and urban slums – is a social history museum located where five shantytowns come together (Aglomerado Santa Lucia), the product of a demand from the community for the right to have their memories respected, as these communities live under the constant threat of being moved out over territorial disputes. This has happened, paradoxically, in the southern part of Belo Horizonte, in the wealthiest part of the city. It is an area where there is considerable real estate speculation. As a consequence, there has been a process of gentrification (expulsion of poor people, blacks and other undesirables from those areas coveted by large commercial enterprises) and of the denial of the rights of the poor to be in the city, their lives. Two of the five shantytowns have already been dismantled, their houses destroyed, their links broken, their stories silenced. The other shantytowns in the Aglomerado face the same threat of total destruction.

The Muquifu arose from Afro-Brazilian resistance to the pernicious logic of market forces and necropolitics. It was established as place where local stories could be told and the ancestral memories of the black people nurtured. In the words of Father Mauro da Silva the co-founder and leader of the Muquifu:

The Muquifu, has the transformation of the territory where it is located as one of its aims. The museum came about through the community's demand for the right that its memories be respected. [The shantytown community wanted] to tell an alternative story, not the one that others have told us, history seen from a white perspective in which, supposedly, our enslaved forebears were totally passive when they were captured in Africa and transported [....]. We weary of not being able to recognise ourselves in the museums we visit which only tell the story of black people in terms of the pain we have suffered; we look for other ways of representing us and the places where we live.[25]

The aim of the Muquifu is to "guarantee the recognition and protection of the shantytowns, the true Brazilian urban quilombos". The peoples of the Aglomerado were invited to tell their stories and leave in the Muquifu some object linked to the course of their lives that was both significant and important: photographs, possessions, pictures of festivities, dances, celebrations, musical instruments, recipes and stories which represented the cultural traditions and lives of the residents. This led to the creation of the first archival collections of material and oral material in this unconventional museum.

The Igreja das Santas Pretas is on the same site as the Muquifu, probably the first anti-racist and depatriarchalised Church. It is far and away the most original manifestation of Afro-Brazilian spiritual resistance within Christian Catholicism. This Church is the realisation of the dream of a group of fourteen black women from the shantytown who sought a "proper church". For these women the shack where, from the 1960's they had cooked, chatted, sewed, took tea and prayed was not a "proper church". Certainly, what they aspired to was a space that had some appearance of a religious edifice.

So, in the midst of life's daily struggles and confrontation with the power of patriarchal clergy, the shantytown black women gave birth to the "proper church" of which they had dreamed. This true Church is embodied in the history of the community and which is portrayed iconographically. From June 2016 a huge fresco measuring a total of 107 square metres is under way which will ultimately cover all the walls of the Igreja das Santas Pretas. The artists undertaking the work are Cleiton Gos and Marcial

Ávila. All the iconography is black in that all the personages depicted are black because, essentially, it is a black community.

The painting creates a parallel link between the fourteen black women who founded the community and the life of Mary, mother of Jesus. Fourteen scenes are depicted covering Mary's seven sorrows and seven joys because the community had learned to tell tales of horror mingled with those of hope.

The Igreja das Santas Pretas is thus, the Church where black women can rediscover the *imago Dei* that the racist system so much wanted to disfigure. Not only the women but also the men are able to recover their *imago Dei* there. Father Mauro himself, a black man, tells how he became black after he was appointed as the pastor of this community. This leads me to believe that the Igreja das Santas Pretas is a Brazilian Church that gives form to the black face of divinity.

In the Igreja das Santas Pretas, the Christian faith is celebrated in perfect harmony with the devotions of Africa. The Congado (Afro-Brazilian celebration mixing African and Brazilian traditions. Trans.), those who take part, the devotion to our Lady of Rosario, harking back to an object of adoration in Africa pre-dating the slave transportation, make up some of the elements of this Church's spiritual resistance. Not only the iconography, the ecclesiology, the sacramentology, the liturgy and, essentially, every structural aspect of the Igreja das Santas Pretas bear witness that something new is happening here: the birth of a new vision for humanity in which the black person celebrates his blackness as a gift.

VI Closing considerations
The process of becoming black is the very nucleus of the theology of the quilombo, allowing the recovery of a black personage as a place of divine manifestation, where our ancestry can be rediscovered and we can construct our Afro-Brazilian identity. The theology of the quilombo is committed ethically, politically and spiritually to the recovery of the *imago Dei* by black men and women and all those nameless victims of global capitalism's systemic approach.

Pivotal in the theology of the quilombo is re-encountering an ancestral religious experience without a renunciation of the Christian faith. That is to say, for us black men and women, an authentic theology that positions us in a sense of double belonging, like an experience at the extremes, which helps us to perceive the revelation of different faces of God, seeing that our own liberation is also a liberation from idolisation [One God, male, white and Eurocentric]. To this end, and within the context of Brazil, the liberation of the black people must also necessarily shape the black face of the Church such that a depatriarchal, anti-racist Christianity becomes manifest.

Translated by Christopher Lawrence

Bibliography

Castro-Gómez, Santiago; Grosfoguel, Ramón (Orgs). *El giro decolonial: reflexiones para una diversidad epistémica más allá del capitalismo global*. Bogotá: Siglo del Hombre Editores, 2007.

Caldeira, Cleusa. "Teologia negra: a fenomenologia do damné como caminho de humanização" in *Revista Horizonte*, 2019.

Fanon, Franz. *Pele negra, máscaras brancas*. Salvador: EDUFBA, 2008.

Mbembe, Achille. *Necropolítica. Seguido de Sobre el gobierno privado indirecto*. España: Melusina, 2011.

Mbembe, Achille. *Crítica da razão negra*. São Paulo: N-1 edições, 2018.

Mbembe, Achille. *Políticas da inimizade*. Lisboa: Antígona, 2017.

Nascimento, Abdias. *O Quilombismo. Documentos de uma militância Pan-Africana*. São Paulo: Ed. Perspectiva, 2019.

Nascimento, Abdias. *O genocídio do negro brasileiro. Processos de um racismo mascarado*. São Paulo: Perspectiva, 2016, p. 111.

Nascimento, Beatriz. "O conceito de quilombo e a resistência cultural negra" in *Afrodiaspora* RJ (1995), Ano 3, n. 6-7, p. 41-49.

Quijano, Aníbal. "*Colonialidad del poder y clasificacion social*". In: Castro-Gómez, Santiago; Grosfoguel, Ramón (Orgs). *El giro decolonial: reflexones para una diversidad epistémica más allá del capitalismo global*. Bogotá: Siglo del Hombre Editores; Universidad Central, Instituto de Estudios Sociales Contemporáneos y Pontifícia Universidad Javeriana, Instituto Pensar, 2007, p. 93-126

Schwarcz, Lilia Moritz. "O espetáculo da miscigenação" en *Estudos*

Avançados 8, 1994, 137-152.
Souza, Neusa Santos. Tornar-se negro ou As vicissitudes da identidade do negro brasileiro em ascensão social. 1983.
Moura, Clóvis. Sociologia do negro brasileiro. São Paulo: 1988.
Moura, Clóvis. "A quilombagem como expressão de protesto radical" en Moura, C. (Org.) *Os quilombos na dinâmica social do Brasil.* Maceió: EDUFAL, 2001.
Silva, Mauro. "*Habemus Muquifu*: Análise da criação e das coleções do Museu dos Quilombos e Favelas Urbanos". Dissertação de mestrado em Ciências Sociais Defendida na PUCMG em 2018.

Notes

Translator's note: A *quilombo* from the Kimbundu word *kilombo*, "war camp" is a Brazilian settlement founded by people of African origin. Most of the inhabitants of quilombos were escaped slaves.

1. See: Atlas da Violência 2019
2. Nascimento, Abdias. O Quilombismo. *Documentos de uma militância Pan-Africana.* São Paulo: Ed. Perspectiva; Rio de Janeiro: Ipeafro, 2019, p. 273-312. Quilombismo: a scientific socio-historical concept coined by Abdias Nascimento to describe the complex significance and *praxis* of quilombo.
3. Fanon, Franz. *Pele negra, máscaras brancas.* Salvador: EDUFBA, 2008, p. 26.
4. Quijano, Aníbal. "Colonialidad del poder y clasificacion social". en: Castro-Gómez, Santiago; Grosfoguel, Ramón (Orgs). *El giro decolonial: reflexones para una diversidad epistémica más allá del capitalismo global.* Bogotá: Siglo del Hombre Editores; Universidad Central, Instituto de Estudios Sociales Contemporáneos y Pontifícia Universidad Javeriana, Instituto Pensar, 2007, p. 93-126.
5. Mbembe, Achille. *Necropolítica seguido de Sobre el gobierno privado indirecto.* España: Melusina, 2011.
6. Mbembe, Achille. *Necropolítica*, 2011.
7. Schwarcz, Lilia Moritz. "O espetáculo da miscigenação" in *Estudos Avançados* 8 (1994) p. 137-152.
8. Nascimento, Abdias. *O genocídio do negro brasileiro. Processos de um racismo mascarado.* São Paulo: Perspectiva, 2016, p. 111.
9. Fanon, Franz. *Pele negra*, 2008, p.188.
10. Souza, Neusa Soura. *Tornar-se negro ou As vicissitudes da identidade do negro brasileiro em ascensão social.* 1983, p. 8.
11. Souza, Neusa Sousa. *Tornar-se negro*, p. 5.
12. Fanon, Franz. Pele Negra, p. 31.
13. Caldeira, Cleusa. "Teologia negra: a fenomenologia do damné como caminho de humanização" en *Revista Horizonte*, 2019.
14. Mbembe, Achille. *Crítica da razão negra.* São Paulo: N-1 edições, 2018, p. 263-307.
15. Moura, Clóvis. "A quilombagem como expressão de protesto radical" en Moura, C.

(Org.) *Os quilombos na dinâmica social do Brasil*. Maceió: EDUFAL, 2001.
16. Nascimento, Beatriz. "O conceito de quilombo e a resistência cultural negra" em *Afrodiaspora* RJ (1995), Ano 3, n. 6-7, p.41-49.
17. Moura, Clóvis. *Sociologia do negro brasileiro*. São Paulo: 1988, p. 159.
18. Nascimento, Beatriz. *O conceito de quilombo*, p.41-49.
19. Ibid.
20. Nascimento, Abdias. *O Quilombismo*, p. 282.
21. Ibid.
22. Mbembe, Achille. *Políticas da inimizade*. Lisboa: Antígona, 2017, p. 185, [our italics].
23. Souza, Neusa Sousa. *Tornar-se negro*, p . 77.
24. Silva, Mauro. "*Habemus* Muquifu: Analysis of the creation and collections of the Museu dos Quilombos e Favelas Urbanos". Masters in Social Science dissertation, presented at PUCMG, in 2018. "The acronym *Muquifu* records the word *muquifo*, which could be a shack in a slum or in a deprived areaque. In a positive connotation, the expression can represent a special place, as for example in saying : This is my *muquifo*, or even, this is my favourite spot". The descriptive information of Muquifu and the Igrejas das Santas Pretas come both from Father Mauro's dissertation and my conversations with him, as well as from my own visits.
25. Silva, Mauro. "*Habemus* Muquifu", p. 141.

Diverse Communities Inhabited by the Divine Ruah

JOSÉ DE JESÚS LEGORRETA ZEPEDA

The wide-ranging and many-faceted debate about community and the commons in social movements, peoples and churches in the global South has turned into a condemnation of and, at the same time, a form of resistance to, the logic of capitalism, which is bereft of solidarity and destructive of community in modern society. Nevertheless, here as well we see emerging new forms of community that broaden and consolidate the utopia of those who believe that 'a different world is possible'. Theologically, then, it is reasonable to ask if this plurality of searches in which the poor, the excluded and the vulnerable resist are other sites of epiphany, where new and unprecedented forms of life in the Spirit are emerging.

I The 'communitarian symptom' as a condemnation and building block of the future

While the sense of individualism is broadly established over large areas of contemporary societies, experiences of and references to community have not disappeared; on the contrary, they have proliferated increasingly in many different environments and senses, whether as a longing for a 'natural' form of life, made up of closeness, warmth and solidarity, or as a defensive, alternative image of life in contexts in which conviviality has been broken, but also, and especially in lower-status and damaged groups who cling to life and produce alternative forms of sociability and resistance to face the logic of the capitalist market, individualist fragmentation and many other forms of violence.

It is important to point out that despite the frequent allusions to community life in the talk and rhetoric of many groups, movements and individuals, not everyone is talking about the same thing. For example, in social sciences 'community' has been a heuristic expression used frequently to refer to ways of life based on ties of intimacy and trust, as opposed to a model of integration and belonging that is impersonal, functional and organic.[1] In the field of philosophy, 'community' is usually thought of as an experience of disappropriation, as a constantly changing external condition, more than as of an institution or a set of individuals who by merging create a larger subject common to all.[2] In contrast, in political language 'communal' tends to be used to refer to groups or collectivities with shared economic or cultural interests or – in a more populist approach – to refer to a set of 'users', 'recipients' or 'clients' of government programmes or projects. Over against these utilitarian and instrumentalising attitudes to community, there is also a common account of community in outlying and lower-class neighbourhoods in the South such that their understanding of themselves as communities has helped them to express alternative ways of life to the various forms of exclusion and violence they face as a matter of routine.[3] Finally, we cannot ignore the frequent presence of community language in many religious traditions, especially Christianity, where groups of believers' sense of themselves as communities has been regarded for centuries as an intrinsic element of their core identity and mission.

This wide and deep semantic field is not a product of the abundance of the conviviality it refers to, but precisely the opposite. It is some years ago that Eric Hobsbawm remarked: 'Never was the word "community" used more indiscriminately and emptily than in the decades when communities in the sociological sense became hard to find in real life.'[4] If this is the case, we need to ask why. A rapid review of some current analyses of the topic give us helpful clues for working out a response.[5] For example, Zygmunt Bauman has pointed out that the process of individuation in modern capitalism reviled and destroyed the pre-modern community network and inserted individuals into the productivist logic of the market in the form of an *ad hoc* sociality that presupposed legal equality and individuality as basic elements.[6] In recent years, Baumann argued, the solid modernity in which this type of sociality emerged has undergone a process of liquefaction in which the supposed solidity of beliefs, institutions, standards of meaning and ways of life in modernity have 'melted', that is, they have become unstable, changeable, amorphous and intangible – this is 'liquid modernity'.[7] In this way not only have the traditional forms of community broken down; the community myth of the nation-state has also evaporated. From now on, suggests Bauman, there is no possibility of reconstructing this lost community except as a tyrannical 'community'.[8] The result is that the emerging world is not welcoming and safe, but hostile and competitive, one in which the main beneficiaries have been the 'successful'.[9] For these, says Bauman, the community that binds and requires sharing is an obstacle insofar as it represents a risk of losing everything.[10] This is why the typical post-modern communities of this sector are preponderantly emotional in type, or 'peg communities', that is, ephemeral, changing communities with no moral responsibility.[11] Using different theoretical references, notably the history of culture, decolonial studies from recent decades, especially in Latin America, have stressed that the 'modernity/coloniality' project initiated in the 16th century imposed a worldwide model of capitalist power that, through colonial domination and the liberal nation-state model, disrupted the first peoples' forms of sociality.[12] Nevertheless, despite these attacks, modernity/coloniality was unable totally to disrupt the inherited forms of community life. The survival of these traditions today provides alternative sources of experience, visions of the world and ways of life that offer a critique of the structures of capitalist sociality.[13] One of the examples of these ideas given most emphasis are the indigenous communities. In addition to these groups, emerging forms of action and reconstruction of community links have grown up in groups and individuals whose social fabric has been damaged or broken by exclusion, insecurity, poverty, forced migration, organised crime and impunity, among other causes.[14] One relevant factor is that this wide spectrum of violence does not affect all types of groups and individuals indiscriminately, but preponderantly vulnerable and lower-status sectors, which makes it reasonable to talk of intentional action by a system that is intrinsically excluding and violent towards the least protected. The points made above lead to the conclusion that the superabundance of community language acts, on the one hand, as a narrative that condemns the breakdown of the violent and individualistic sociality, lacking in solidarity, created by capitalist society (like the 'community myth' that bases society on an essence, on the spirit of a people, a race or a destiny);[15] on the other hand, it acts as an appeal to and defence of emancipatory and alternative life-styles. In Latin America this utopia that is being constructed laboriously in peoples and organisations in resistance is usually given labels such as 'living well' or 'living well together' or 'honourably present'.

Finally, it is important to stress that this *sensus communis* or general feeling has shown that there is no natural form or universal model of community, but that community is a socio-cultural product and while in the West it has been associated with ideas such as equality, selfhood and harmony, today forms of community are emerging with different make-ups, unstable, fleeting and multiple.[16]

II And Christian *community?*

The great majority of religious traditions have proclaimed community to be an inherent feature of their identity. In the Christian tradition, for example, community and Church have been identified for centuries and have been so important that God himself has been understood as a 'community God' (Trinity). In the last 50 years the community dimension of the Church has experienced a vigorous rebirth as a result of the renewed attention paid to the ecclesiology of the Church as mystery developed in the first millennium and the theological idea of the Church as the people of God at the Second Vatican Council. Since then no treatise on ecclesiology has failed to mention community. Nonetheless it is symptomatic that the majority of these ecclesiologies are full of complex and erudite theological disquisitions about communion as the foundation and source of community, but neglect to discuss community itself and say what they mean by it. This absence is ambivalent in that, one the one hand it is positive to leave open the possibility of specifying how life in common can be traced in history and understood, but, on the other hand, the omission also allows for the legitimation of the status quo, in which Church community is simply identified with the current institutional arrangements of the Church, which are not at all indeterminate or abstract. This last position, predominant in recent centuries, suffers from some serious problems; for example, it has it has led to a situation in which it is taken for granted on the institutional and doctrinal level, and in the popular imagination, that there is only one form of 'Christian community', which is identified with the institutional complex of the Church (universalist, monarchical, uniform and hierarchical). This legal 'mono-ecclesiocentrism' has restricted internally the recognition of alternative forms of Church life that do not precisely follow the prescriptions of canon law, while in its position towards the outside world the model has difficulty has recognising Church features in communities whose constitution and dynamic is not defined in advance as a church or religious movement. Finally, another serious problem is that the model in question is today barely plausible, since the specific forms of community in which it operates were designed in a premodern sociocultural setting in which the dominant community logic was *reductio ad unum* and in which membership was not by choice but by obligatory and exclusive admission. None of this would be so much of a problem if the Church model in question followed a model or archetype of common life prescribed by Jesus, but this is just what we do not have. Biblical research of the last 50 years has shown that no binding model of community can be derived from Jesus or the first Christians. What we do find in the origins is a plurality of attempts at social organisation to live the experience of faith based on Jesus as a Church, adopting and adapting forms of membership and interaction dominant in specific contexts.

At this point it would not be surprising for the question to be asked whether, through a reaction to an ecclesiological docetism implicit in the earlier account, we are not falling into the precise opposite, a sort of sociologism. Here it is appropriate to explain that the Church does not exist as a body apart from the believers: 'The Church is not the *Ecclesia de Trinitate* except as an *Ecclesia ex hominibus*.'[17] If the Church is the People of God, the Body of Christ, the temple of the Spirit, it is all this as a human reality where revelation occurs and whose experience is shared intersubjectively in a group. As a result, the object of ecclesiology cannot be simply theological reflection about the Church, but also the historical reality in which it manifests itself as a social reality.[18]

To sum up, at the crux of the debate about community set out earlier it is of vital importance to believers to ask themselves if their experience of faith can only be lived in those inherited pre-modern forms, or whether it is already being recreated, through the action of the Spirit, in the emerging forms of sociality that interweave movements, groups and individuals in their vulnerability to resist in contexts of violence.

III Communities of faith, resistance and *dignified futures* inhabited by the Spirit

According to some studies, violence as we know it today (the patriarchal state, war and exploitation of nature), appeared about six million years ago, a product of the use and exploitation of energy by some elites, through slavery, serfdom and the intensive use of animals for work.[19] Nevertheless, the *current pattern of power and violence* is a relatively recent phenomenon, produced by 'modern or colonial, Euro-centred capitalism'.[20] According to Aníbal Quijano, this *world pattern of power* began with the conquest of America in the 16th century, mediated by two lines of thinking: first, the idea of *race*, through which the hierarchical differences, and differences of roles, skills and culture between (European) conquerors and the conquered were treated as normal because historically and biologically natural, and, second, the organisation of every form of *exploitation of labour* (slavery, serfdom, exchange and wage) around the production of commodities for the 'world' market.[21] The expansion of capitalism, colonialist and Europe-centred, became established as *standard thinking*, doing violence to, subordinating and disrupting everything different from itself, skills, social organisation, cosmologies, conceptions of life and of the divine.[22] In reality, this *world system* (as Wallerstein called it) has revealed is failure through its ecological, political and social unviability to generalise its development project, to allow a diversity of skills, ways of life, world views, standards of meaning and sexual preferences, among other variables, to coexist 'ecologically on equal terms. The various forms of violence resulting from this civilisational collapse have unleashed their full force on the poorest and most vulnerable population groups, that is, the great majority of humanity, sharpening the impact of want, inequality and violence. One of the deeply felt consequences of this destructive force has been the breaking of the social fabric and, finally, the intensification of individualism, lack of solidarity, despoliation, indifference and fear.

Despite this surrounding climate, in the last 30 years social movements, groups and projects have grown up that are tending to reconstruct, reconstitute or create unprecedented networks of social harmony that involve 'the re-establishment of social ties, law and social justice and creation of the cultural, environmental and structural conditions for social harmony'.[23] In short, rather than *reconstruction*, this is participatory *construction*, of life-styles based on solidarity, mutual care and care of the surroundings designed to promote the emergence of life-styles that are emancipatory and alternative to the worldwide model of hegemonic power.

From a theological point of view we may ask whether this multiplicity of searches in which poor, excluded and vulnerable people resist and survive the present context of violence are not so many *sites of epiphany*, where unprecedented forms of life in the Spirit are emerging, where control by a particular religious system or institution stops.[24] From a faith perspective we need to watch out for these signs of the times, where the *Breath of God as Spirit* in history reveals itself as it calls into being more dignified and more just life-styles.

In many of these groups and projects for the *reconstruction of the social fabric* in contexts of violence that have appeared in Latin America, a sort of *conversion* is taking place, from a mercantile, utilitarian, fragmented and individualistic attitude to reality to an attitude based on an ecosystem in which human degradation (poverty, exclusion and violence) is correlative to and interdependent with environmental degradation. That is why various projects for repairing the social fabric are being associated with a renewal of ties, not only with other people, but also with the earth, with collective memory, with other forms of knowledge and with the ecological setting in general. This other 'way of looking' may be understood as a 'spirituality' that envisages more than 'reality' in the singular, *multiple realities*, all connected and connecting, part of a *pluriverse* that in an important Christian tradition has been expressed through the metaphor of the 'common home'. This ecological conversion of our way of looking at things, as Pope Francis called it in *Laudato Si'*,[25] implies profound changes in the life-styles and in power structures in which society is organised, the production and operation of institutions, including religious ones. That is why the presence of God as Spirit will have to be discerned in the multifarious emergence of communities, movements and groups that resist and survive the predatory logic of capitalism, while at the same time practising emancipatory forms of life and interrelation.

Recognising and making visible these diverse communities inhabited by the divine *Ruah* will in future imply a wide-ranging and long-term task, analogous to that proposed by Boaventura de Sousa Santos when he talks about a sociology of what is emerging. For the subject of community with which we are concerned here, we can paraphrase Santos' words and talk of an ecclesiology of emergent communities that takes as its aim detecting and recovering the expectations expressed and latent in the diversity of emerging experiences of community in which, also, new spiritualities are being revealed.

Translated by Francis McDonagh

Bibliography

Bauman, Zygmunt, Community. *Seeking Safety in an Insecure World*, Cambridge and Malden MA, 2001

Esposito, Roberto. *Communitas, origen y destino de la comunidad*, Buenos Aires: Amorrortu, 2003.

Hobsbawm, Eric. *The Age of Extremes*, London: Abacus, 1994.

Komonchak, Joseph A. 'Ecclesiology and Social Theory: A Methodological Essay', *The Thomist* 45 (1981), 268-269.

Legorreta, José de J. 'Cuando la comunidad no a-cumuna: Debates contemporáneos sobre la "falla" del estar-en-común', *En-claves del pensamiento*, 11/22 (2017), 75-107.

Pope Francis, Encyclical *Laudato Si'. On Care for our Common Home*, 24 May 2015: http://www.vatican.va/content/francesco/en/encyclicals/documents/papa-francesco_20150524_enciclica-laudato-si.html [Accessed 18/01/20].

Quijano, Aníbal. 'Colonialidad del poder, eurocentrismo y América latina' en E. Lander (comp.), *La colonialidad del saber: eurocentrismo y ciencias sociales. Perspectivas latinoamericanas*. Buenos Aires: CLACSO 2000, pp. 201-246.

Santos, Boaventura. *Epistemologies of the South: Justice against Epistemicide*. London and New York: Routledge/Taylor and Francis, 2016.

Torres, Alfonso. *El retorno a la comunidad. Problemas, debates y desafíos de vivir en común*. Bogotá: El Búho, 2014.

Notes

1. Pablo de Marinis, 'Sociología clásica y comunidad: entre la nostalgia y la utopía', in Pablo de Marinis, Gabriel Gatti, Ignacio Irazuzta (ed.), *La comunidad como pretexto. En torno al (re) surgimiento de las solidaridades comunitarias*, Barcelona, 2010, p. 356.
2. A general view of these philosophies is given by Mónica B. Cragnolini, M. B. (Ed.), 'Extrañas comunidades: para una metafísica del exilio', in: *Extrañas comunidades. La impronta nietzscheana en el debate contemporáneo*, Buenos Aires, 2009, pp 51-64. Some of the most relevant philosophical texts on community are: Jean-Luc Nancy, *La comunidad inoperante*, Santiago de Chile, 2000; Roberto Esposito, *Communitas, origen y destino de la comunidad*, Buenos Aires, 2003; Giorgio Agamben, *The Coming Community*, Minneapolis, MN, 1993.
3. Cf Alfonso Torres, *El retorno a la comunidad. Problemas, debates y desafíos de vivir en común*, Bogotá, 2014, especially Chap. 7.
4. Eric Hobsbawm, *The Age of Extremes*, London, 1994, p. 428.
5. There is a summary of the ideas of some contemporary thinkers about community in

José J. Legorreta, 'Cuando la comunidad no a-cumuna: Debates contemporáneos sobre la "falla" del estar-en-común', *En-claves del pensamiento*, 11/22 (2017), 75-107; Gerard Delanty, *Community. Comunidad, educación ambiental y ciudadanía*, Barcelona, 2006.
6. Zygmunt Bauman, *Community. Seeking Safety in an Insecure World*, Cambridge and Malden MA, 2001, pp. 21-38.
7. Zygmunt Bauman, *Liquid Modernity*, Cambridge and Malden MA, 2000, pp 2-4.
8. Zygmunt Bauman, *Community*, pp 7-20.
9. Bauman, pp 50-51.
10. Bauman, pp 52-53.
11. Bauman, pp 70-73.
12. Aníbal Quijano, 'Colonialidad y Modernidad / Racionalidad', *Perú Indígena* 13 (1992), 11-20.
13. Alfonso Torres, *El retorno a la comunidad. Problemas, debates y desafíos de vivir en común*, Bogotá 2014, p. 15.
14. In the last two decades Latin American studies on these emerging forms of collective action have approached the issue through the metaphor of 'social fabric'. Cf Yuri A. Chávez & Uva Falla 'Realidades y falacias de la reconstrucción del tejido social en población desplazada', *Tabula Rasa* 2 (2004), 169-187; Gabriel Mendoza & Jorge González, *Reconstrucción del tejido social: una apuesta por la paz*, Mexico City:, 2016.
15. Cf Ander Gurrutxaga, 'El redescubrimiento de la comunidad', *Revista Española de Investigaciones Sociológicas* 56 (1991), 35-60.
16. Gabriela Vargas, 'La asociación efímera. Repensando el concepto de comunidad desde la literatura cyberpunk', *Cuadernos de Bioética* (11), sección doctrina. Available at: http://uady.academia.edu/GabrielaVargasCetina [Accessed 17/01/20]; Pablo De Marinis, '16 comentarios sobre la(s) sociología(s) y la(s) comunidad(es)', Papeles del CEIC,15 (2005) 1-39.
17. Joseph A. Komonchak, 'Towards a Theology of the Local Church', *FABC Papers* 42 (1986), 9.
18. Joseph A. Komonchak, 'Ecclesiology and Social Theory: A Methodological Essay', *The Thomist* 45 (1981), 268-269.
19. Cf Ramón Fernández and Luis González, *En la espiral de la Energía*, v. I, Madrid, 2018, p. 77.
20. Aníbal Quijano, 'Colonialidad del poder, eurocentrismo y América latina' in: E. Lander (ed.), *La colonialidad del saber: eurocentrismo y ciencias sociales. Perspectivas latinoamericanas*, Buenos Aires, 2000, pp. 201-246.
21. Aníbal Quijano, 'Colonialidad del poder, eurocentrismo y América latina', pp 202-205.
22. For a systematic overview of these modern capitalist logic of treating what is different as inferior, see Boaventura de Sousa Santos, *Epistemologies of the South. Justice against Epistemicide*, Boulder, CO, and London, 2014, pp 99-101.
23. Gabriel Mendoza and Jorge González, *Reconstrucción del tejido social: una apuesta por la paz*, Mexico City, 2016, p. 25.
24. Cf Juan J. Tamayo and Raúl Fornet-Betancourt, *Interculturalidad, diálogo interreligioso y liberación. I Simposio Internacional de Teología Intercultural e Interreligiosa de la Liberación*, Estella, 2005. For an explanatory overview of the relationships between community and spiritualities, see *Polis. Revista Latinoamericana: Espiritualidad y comunidad* 8 (2004).
25. Pope Francis, Encyclical *Laudato Si'. On Care for our Common Home*, 24 May 2015: http://www.vatican.va/content/francesco/en/encyclicals/documents/papa-francesco_20150524_enciclica-laudato-si.html [Accessed 18/01/20].

Acts of Resistance: Messianic Force of Divine Anarchy

JUAN CARLOS LA PUENTE TAPIA

Starting from stories of resistance that store the mystery of human dignity, the article examines the changes taking place, as signs of hope, in the contexts of global violence. It analyses a change in the quality of time, combined with an epistemological and anthropological change, that constitutes and invitation to be received in the depths of the wounds existing in the nowhere of cycles of domination, condemnation and sacrifice in order to receive there the messianic force of redemption.

I Voices and provocations
A voice from Colombia
'Why does a group of a few families want to stay on land so fiercely disputed and under pressure from armed groups?' Aren't they being offered a whole package of incentives to move? The question came from a high-ranking foreign diplomat in Colombia. The answer was immediate. Emilio told him: 'Our resistance is our way of living with dignity.'

A voice from the United States
I was invited to a farewell dinner for Javier, to whom, like millions of other people, the laws of the legal and political system of many countries, deny official documentation. He is prevented from obtaining residence to publicly exercise the right to defend his rights.

Javier was suffering from a terminal illness and could not walk. He was in a wheelchair. With difficulty he told me: 'I'm going to my country to die; that's why we're having the dinner.' Juana, his wife, told me with a smile: 'It's a goodbye party. Thank you for coming. I hope you like the food.' David, their eldest child, had been born in the United States and so, at the age of 16, could go with his father to the land he had come from, where he wanted to die, and then go back to Oregon. David didn't know if he would be able to stay to see his father live out his last days there or perhaps would have to leave him and come back straight away. His father would die without seeing Juana and his two younger children. Friends begged him: 'Javier, have faith. You can get well and stay with your family. It makes no sense to leave.'

Javier started to speak. 'What point does my life have if not to show my daughters, my son and my wife our dignity?' He added: 'If they have faith, they ought to understand that dying with dignity reflects a life lived with dignity. My country is calling me, and I'm returning to it with dignity.'

The people praying gradually fell silent as Javier looked at them. María, a neighbour, said: 'Brother, your children are my children. Where there's food for three, there's food for six. I don't know how, but don't worry: we are here supporting Juana, David and your other children.' Other people joined in; another prayer rose from hearts emboldened by having seen their own dignity reflected in Javier.

Someone knelt down and asked for a blessing from Javier and his family. Many of us followed suit and asked them to give us strength to live with dignity in the midst of the horror of thousands of deportations and family separations. From his wheelchair, Javier touched out heads with his hand while we hugged him and his family. We had been introduced – or rather, enlightened, born – into a communal Presence that revealed resistance, dignity and the fulness of liberation.

A voice from Mexico
'Why do you keep searching if all the signs are that your son is dead? Why do you run such a risk by denouncing the inefficiency and corruption of that state bureaucracy if in the end, when all is said and done, you know perfectly well that your son is dead?' Rosario replied: 'If you knew the power of God that gives me strength. The power of God is a light different from all the signs you mention; it's a light that lets you see the disappeared people that others can't see. It's that light that helps me to go on searching, not just for my son, but for thousands.'

Seduced by the mystery of human dignity preserved by webs of resistance in contexts of global violence, I met Rosario and she told me about her struggle and the various objections she had faced from family and friends. Among other things, she said: 'As well, I can tell you this: after so much love my family was able to understand that love changes the calendar and changes time. For example, now we'll be having Christmas when I get back from a march with other women. We've celebrated my grand-daughters' birthdays when we've been able to, after journeys in solidarity with other women who, like me, are looking for their disappeared daughters and sons. Time has been transformed by the love I feel for my son.'

II A change in perception: listening, friendship and communion with the open wounds on our bodies

Listening to the voices of the victims is crucial if we want to think about how we recognise ourselves in other people's acts of resistance. The construction of knowledge has as its starting point listening to each other, rooted in a deep inter-subjective relationship; otherwise, how would we know that our hearts had met when we listened to each other? How would we know that our acts of resistance don't conflict with each other?

Listening and deep relationship have to go together and their destination is friendship, where the listening touches and is touched, where our acts of resistance are recognised and become interwoven with many other acts of resistance. At the hearth of friendship relationships open their most intimate pores and in this way the acts of resistance that we are engaged in can be interwoven through a mutual recognition in the vulnerability of our open wounds.

In this sense the change in perception of which we are a part reveals a way in which we construct forms of knowledge that could not exist without these three roots: listening, friendship and communion with the open wounds that mark our bodies. In the same way these roots allow us to have a dialogue that generates languages that broaden our capacities for talking about new worlds, new heavens that we experience, which awaken and sustain our resistances.

III An anthropological change: friendship in Life[1]

Our starting point is the warning we have heard in our acts of resistance against the identitarian traps that encourage us to fight over who has the better title to humanity or divinity in order to control the lives and deaths of others.

There are experiences that do not fight the dominant systems over identity or power. Acts of resistance shelter experiences in their depths that generate new ways of living that the dominant systems are unaware of or have not yet been able to control, those that collectively illuminate care for Life in the areas of education, health, production and care for one another.

Deconstructing religious identity as a refuge of purity based on the sacrifice of other identities is also a call to interweave acts of resistance. This opens up a perspective in which 'religious friendship' between people on different spiritual journeys or different traditions places us on alert for attempts at synthesis, uniformity and control through identitarian traps. In spiritual friendship there is a mutual transformation through care for the wisdom of the different paths that humanity has been preserving to care for Life. To be friends of Life is the basis of care for Life, the blazing core of the friendship we are talking about.[2] Friendship transforms us more and more into friends of life until we become Life itself in friendship.

Care for Life and friendship are two fundamental dimensions that are nourishing the resistance movements.

III A change in the quality of time: acts that are creative, transgressive and symbolic

The experiences of resistance reveal a dynamism in reality that occurs outside the calculations that the systems of domination and condemnation allow as tools for survival. Chronological time, on this view, is associated with the survival calculus within the systems of domination and condemnation. What we are talking about here is a change in the quality of time as the creation of what the same systems of oppression in their malign predictions never believed possible, a transgression of time.

Acts of resistance show the marks of an *alternative* time, a creative resistance that kicks over the toolbox offered by the patriarchal, colonial and individualist systems. They beat with a freedom that transcends the calculus of oppression and invite us to slip through cracks into new sorts of time, through *symbolic acts and forms of creative resistance*. The web of acts of resistance seeks not so much vengeance on the executioners, since that would only reflect our captivity in ordinary time, but tries to ensure that there are no more atrocities; it creates new gestures that embody something unknown to the systems of oppression, forgiveness offered as a breach in time. In this sense, acts of resistance recall, bring about and anticipate new worlds. They are actions that incarnate the ancestral body, not only the bodies of those sacrificed by oppressive systems, but also those of the executioners whose cries beg for forgiveness. They are actions that bring about the healing of the ancestral body and which only after they are performed in the here and now – hidden from all calculation under the eyes of the oppressive systems – anticipate in celebration the remembrance yearned for by all generations, including those to come. It is acts of resistance and transgression that produce this change in the quality of time. Even when they are not valued by the systems of oppression as instruments of discussion in any possible negotiation, when they are performed they remove the obstacles that hid from view new possible destinations.

Celebration and festivals, with singing and dancing and sharing of food, are symbols of the deconstruction of the trapped calculus offered by the systems of domination and condemnation and the organisations that survive within the range of permitted teachings. It is here that we celebrate the life we are already living in the web of our resistances, now and as a longed for future. We celebrate not having been the prey of the dream offered by the systems of domination and condemnation.

Imprisoned by the systems of oppression, we used to calculate and reason in terms of the prejudices and information that are a by-product of those very systems. In contrast, when we talk about creation, we are talking about being surprised by something that we could never even have been prejudiced about. It is the new world. And this creation is experienced in the form of poetry that makes possible a new imagination out of our surprise to find ourselves people called upon in the histories of others who are also resisting. All this is a creative force of which we are part. This *original surprise* is at the root of the experience of a different quality of time.

V Vocation
The experiences mentioned here as crucial, and the three changes – in perception, in our view of human nature and in time – that have been

taking place in the web of acts of resistance are an invitation to us to enter into Life itself, freed from the cycle of competing domination and condemnation. They are illuminated at the heart of the acts of resistance as these embody messianic actions springing from wounds that are not denied, but offered by real people as a possibility for all of us to reverse competing processes of domination and condemnation.[3]

From the farthest bounds, beyond where the eyes of the oppressive systems can see, real people show forth the messianic power that inhabits their acts of loving self-giving that reveal a new era. It is an era in which competing emotions of fear and calculation have subsided in people's very bodies, when such people are embraced in friendship and embark on the longed-for reconciliation of the ancestral body that we recognise and experience as the *not yet absence and not yet presence* of the infinite communion that brings us to birth with cries of hope. Beyond all claim to a separate and superior identity,[4] real people enmeshed in the webs of resistance share with others their pain, now communally transfigured as a saving power. In this way reality, laden with wounds at the heart of the web of acts of resistance, brings to birth a mysterious presence and relationship of surprise, grace and healing when real people recognise each other in one another's wounds and are reborn communally through their encounter in a transgression that makes a crack in the chronological time of rivalry.

These wounds, if we receive them and they open to each other, without forming a competing principle, but through the offer of forgiveness, stammer a loving basis for reality that pulsates with *divine an-archy*.[5] It is a foundation without any competing principle, a foundation without foundation, without any pedestal from which a different world can be condemned.

We are talking about the end of all calculation that prevents us from being touched in our wounds and touching the wounds of those of us who have our hearts broken by competing oppression.[6] By being inserted and submerged in others,[7] or better, baptised, we recognise each other mutually, peoples in peoples, and heavens in earths, without beginning and without end,[8] in the blessed abyss of the mystery of *divine an-archy*,[9] as pure detachment, supreme relationality and freedom in which fear has lost all its power (1 Jn 4.18) and, in the end, the superabundance of love rises up as the messianic power that nourishes the heart of our acts of resistance.

VI Summons

The invitation to weave a web of resistances comes from real people who – opening each other's wounds – transfigure that web, so making possible an emerging transgression that challenges and deconstructs relationships of domination and condemnation. Through the courage of those who support this power of messianic anticipation, we receive the invitation to *learn to be received by other people*. In this sense, the invitation is not separated from a *someone* who *makes room to receive others*. And what better example could there be than the mother who *makes space* and invites us to share in Life itself. In this way the fulness of reality is revealed in its most intimate depths: at the edges of the farthest edges, where the systems of oppression have not been able to subdue the mystery of human dignity there beats the divine an-archy that makes space and invites us to be received, to be sons and daughters of Life.[10]

The messianic actions make space for all and sundry, as acts of forgiveness and giving that make space for us. Our *being* is therefore *being that is received in communion as the ancestral body that illuminates us*.[11] We are received into the communion that proclaims the non-absence of those whom the systems of oppression treat as annihilated, and we are received into the friendship that proclaims *the not-yet-presence* of those who will come on various paths of resistance.

But the proclamation of the redemption and forgiveness offered are not unconnected with pain. *Making space* is not unconnected with pain. At its most painful depth, the webs of resistance embody the messianic strength of the *divine an-archy* that makes space, again and again, calling for a new birth for reconciliation. This call is an invitation to each one of us.

By virtue of that source experience of *being received* from the beginning of time and so having no reference point of any sort from which to compete, we receive *being free* of any competing principle. This freedom (faith), inspired by the messianic force of divine an-archy, makes it possible for us to *receive others* (justice) in friendship (charity) committed (hope) to the messianic age. Receiving other people into the depths of the web of our acts of resistance then becomes a powerful invitation in which we find ourselves immersed, through our wounds exposed and offered: body and blood symbolised in the bread and wine that, offered in communion, proclaim and enact the messianic banquet.

Translated by Francis McDonagh

Notes

1. Ivan Illich, 'If in this technological world we still have anything like a political life, it would start with friendship', quoted in Gustavo Esteva, 'Iván Illich para el México de hoy', *Crítica*, Year 1, no. 1. January-June 2016, p. 27: http://www.critica.org.mx/Esteva.pdf [accessed 2 January 2020].
2. 'The decision to make an option for the poor is a decision for the God of life, for the lover of life, as the book of Wisdom puts it (Wis 11.26),' Gustavo Gutiérrez, *¿Dónde dormirán los pobres?*, Lima, 1996. p. 56.
3. This messianism has a very close relationship to the analysis put forward by Carlos Mendoza-Álvarez, in terms of Southern epistemology, of Jesus' messianism and his poetic imagination, and the anti-system and decolonising attitude stemming from the potential of the resilient poor and victims. See Carlos Mendoza-Álvarez, *Deus Ineffabilis. Una teología posmoderna de la revelación del fin de los tiempos*, Barcelona, 2015.
4. Jewish mystical texts remind us that if we abandon the illusion of being 'something separate from something else', we open ourselves to the Life that has no beginning and no end. Cf. Lawrence Kushner, *God was in this place and I, i did not know. Finding self, spirituality and ultimate meaning*, Woodstock VT, 2002, pp 98-99.
5. My inspiration here is the word-play and explorations of the term engaged in by Carlos Mendoza-Álvarez, with reference to the Guha or empty cave in the Syro-Malankara liturgy that the theologian explores, calling it 'the most radical theophany cave that any creature has ever explored'. See Carlos Mendoza-Álvarez, *Travesías Indianas*, Mexico City, 2019, pp 106-117.
6. This is a reinterpretation – in the context of acts of resistance – of the mystical clarity of Raimon Pannikar, who stated that the only possible mediation if we were to open ourselves to the divine mystery was nothing less than our naked existence. Cf Raimon Pannikar, *Iconos del Misterio. La experiencia de Dios*, Barcelona, 2001. p. 31. 'We have to be "nothing" to experience in ourselves the Creator of nothingness.' (p. 154). English edition: *The Experience of God. Icons of the Mystery*, Minneapolis, MN, 2006.
7. 'By being inserted into the process of the liberation of the Latin American people we live the gift of faith, hope and charity that makes us disciples of the Lord. This experience constitutes our joy,' Gustavo Gutiérrez, *Beber en su propio pozo. En el itinerario de un pueblo*, Lima, 1983, pp 13-14. English edition: *We Drink from Our Own Wells*, Maryknoll, NY, 2003, and London, 2005.
8. In harmony with many mystical traditions, we see how our very contingency opens us up to the infinite, and in Christian experience infinity is not separated from the relationality to which the Trinitarian faith invites us: 'This becoming aware that in ourselves we are without beginning and without end is, precisely, the experience of divinity,' Raimon Pannikar, *Iconos del Misterio. La experiencia de Dios*, Barcelona, 2001. p. 163.
9. This is the extreme oxymoron of the path of detachment taught by Meister Eckhart, beautifully expressed by his disciple Juan Taulero in the 14th century: 'Let the abyss of the divine darkness, known only by itself and unknown by all things, enlighten you. This blessed abyss, unknown and nameless, will be more beloved and will attract souls more than all that the saints in blessedness may know of divine being.' It is in this abyss that there takes place the superabundant birth of divine love as pure encounter, pure relatedness. Eckhart expresses it as follows: 'You must plunge your "being you" in his "being him" so that "yours" and "his" becomes a "my-being" through mutual possession in love.' And even more forcefully, John of the Cross exclaims: 'Mine are the heavens and mine is the earth. Mine are the nations. The just are mine, the sinners mine. The angels are mine,

and the Mother of God and all things are mine. And God himself is mine and for me because Christ is mine and all for me.' Quoted from Brian Farrely, 'La "via Eckhardi" como itinerario espiritual para la unión con Dios", *Ciencia Tomista*, No 413, vol. 127 (2000), 361, 374.

10. To give Life might be associated with something imposed that is given to someone. In contrast, here I am trying to put at a distance the sounds of patriarchy and to get close to metaphors and symbols that invite us to the divine generation of Life as making space for otherness and something with which we can be in communion, making space in turn and lighting up new worlds. The Council of Toledo in the 7th century confessed that divine generation took place nowhere else but in the Father's 'womb, …the source and origin of all divinity' (cf Denzinger-Hünermann 526, 525). This gives new meaning to Gustavo Gutiérrez' remark: 'To liberate is, in the last resort, to give Life, all Life' (*Beber en su propio pozo. En el itinerario de un pueblo*, Lima, 1983, p. 12).

11. 'The sage is the person who has the heart of the whole people and Meister Eckhart, repeating a popular belief, says that 'anyone who knows themselves, knows all creatures' (specifically in his treatise On the noble man). This chain uniting everything with everything else makes us one with nature through contemplation, prayer, glory, but also through our participation in the pains of creation, whether pains of birth or despair' (Raimon Pannikar, *Íconos del Misterio. La experiencia de Dios*, p. 135).

Part Four: Theological Forum

From Vatican II to the Synod on Amazonia: Towards a Synodal Church

ALFREDO FERRO MEDINA S J

The 'kairos' we are experiencing in the Church as a result of the Synod on Amazonia is pushing us to travel on new paths in the whole of the Universal Church, inspired by the Spirit that breathed on the synodal process related to a territory like Amazonia and the peoples that live in it. The reality of the Amazon region invites the whole Church to listen carefully to the cries of the territory and its inhabitants and, in turn, stimulates us to a comprehensive conversion in pastoral, ecological, cultural and synodal ways. This challenge is to consolidate a Church that is outward-facing and a Church of presence.

I Introduction

The great novelty of this synod, entitled: 'Amazonia: New Paths for the Church and for a Comprehensive Ecology', was that it set out an ecclesiology that came from a Church journey, suggesting a new way of being Church, established since the Second Vatican Council, on the basis of the idea of a people of God with different Church practices, not only in Amazonia, where this process has been in consolidation as something slow and irreversible.

This model of Church has been criticised by Pope Francis' detractors in connection with the process of the synod. Those who resist change – and cling to sclerotic and outmoded structures and pastoral practices that have outlived their usefulness – are upset when Pope Francis declares that clericalism is like leprosy in the Church, as he did when he listed the fourteen temptations facing the Vatican curia. These problems can also be found in dioceses, parishes or religious congregations. Other people criticise Pope Francis for saying that the Church should be imagined as an inverted pyramid, with the laity at the top and the bishops underneath.[1] That is why we urgently need to move towards polyhedral and synodal model of Church.[2]

In this connection Pope Francis' call in *Evangelii Gaudium* for us to be an 'outgoing Church' (cf EG 20) produces confusion insecurity and fear because it is more comfortable to continue with a ministry of 'conservation' than to promote a ministry of openness and listening to the cries of the poor, the excluded and the vulnerable, those who ask their pastors to journey with them to achieve a liberation that is nowhere to be found.[3]

II Synod as process

It is reasonable to ask why Pope Francis summoned a special synod on Amazonia. The facts are undeniable: there is a territory under threat and peoples dominated and discriminated against as a result of the predatory development model imposed on an area that is strategic for the planet and for humanity. The Church is laying itself open to question about its mission here and now, taking into account the reality and the challenges in the voice and song of the Amazon with the message of life that rises from the cry of the earth and calls us to a total conversion.[4]

The world climate crisis – according to the encyclical *Laudato Si'* with its call for ecological conversion – is a global alert, so serious that it deserved a synodal space for reflection, analysis, deeper examination, meditation and celebration that would allow us to risk journeying and sailing together as a Church, looking for responses and hopes in the midst of the crisis. The synod was not an isolated event. There was a long process of preparation lasting over two years, which became official in Puerto Maldonado, in January 2018, as a result of Pope Francis' visit to Peru, where he met indigenous peoples and started the synodal process for Amazonia. From that moment, the Amazonian Church – working closely with the bishops' conferences, the national and local churches, religious and the Panamazonian Church Network (REPAM) – mobilised to carry out a series of listening sessions through territorial assemblies, thematic forums, meetings and conversation groups, in which about 8,000 people actively participated. The start was a preparatory document, leading to a Working Document. Then in Rome, the Synod produced a

Final Document, intended as the basis for an Apostolic Exhortation from Pope Francis. The Synod's Final Document was the result of a painful labour because it could not please all the synod fathers, to the point that theologian Walter Kasper commented: 'The Pope is disappointing both progressives and conservatives. The extremes meet.'[5] Within the synod hall and in the small working groups it was clear that there was a multiplicity of criteria, ideas, perspectives and options in a Church that is diverse and not monolithic. What was reflected in the comments – and in the voting on each paragraph of the final text – was a wide consensus on the need to move in new directions to reinforce and consolidate a new way of being Church in Amazonian territory. This was the atmosphere that we breathed in the synod, questioning an authoritarian, pyramidal, clerical, self-referential, neo-colonial and patriarchal.

III A call to a synodal conversion of the Church

The synod's Final Document stresses the need for four great conversions: pastoral, ecological, cultural and synodal. All are closely connected and together are a huge challenge, not just for the Church in Amazonia, but for the universal Church.

The pastoral conversion that concerns us pushes us to be an 'outgoing Church' that places at the centre of mission the proclamation of God made by Jesus. We have to be a Church able to listen to the cry of the peoples, putting emphasis on the formation, support and development of missionary Church communities. For this we need a Church with many and varied ministries that recognises the action of the holy Spirit in the leadership of men and women, accepting with joy the sacraments that should not be exclusively in the hands of priests. Communities must live the eucharist, opening the way for the ordination of *viri probati*. It should be stressed that this is mentioned in the context of the eucharist, and not is a suggestion for coping with the shortage of vocations. Clerical proposals were sharply criticised during the presentations of synod participants, in terms of an incarnate, Indian theology that is part of an approach exploring Amazonian rites.

Only a Church that makes a preferential option for the indigenous and is in dialogue with local cultures – with new rites, symbols, signs and expressions – will be able to express faith in the presence of the Lord in the midst of these peoples' culture, bringing together faith and life.

IV An outgoing Church, Samaritan and prophetic in defence of and care for life

If we prefer what pope Francis has described as 'a Church which is bruised, hurting and dirty because it has been out on the streets, rather than a Church which is unhealthy from being confined and from clinging to its own security' (*Evangelii Gaudium*, 49), then we must rethink our presence among the communities, and our pastoral practices and educational programmes, whether in catechetics or in the formation of pastoral workers, ministers and seminarians, so that we really respond to specific realities of mission in the Amazonian context.

Only a Church that is Samaritan, prophetic and defends the rights of the poorest and the persecuted will be able to bear witness to Jesus. If we are to serve the Amazonian communities, we will have to challenge the often corrupt powers that plunder their resources and threaten their lives and culture. That means watching public policies to influence them, paying attention to the flows of migration and the lives of the indigenous, rural communities, Afro-descendant people, young people, the inhabitants of the outskirts of the cities and, in general, the damaged. We need to support, and let ourselves be supported by, our communities and peoples to open up areas for participation, making proposals in the perspective of wisdom and 'living well'.

In short, I believe that the Spirit of the Lord descended on the Synod for Amazonia, as it did on the Church at its birth on the day of Pentecost, and that that Spirit will never abandon the Church, but will continue to enlighten it.

Translated by Francis McDonagh

Notes

1. Pope Francis, Address at the commemoration of the 50th anniversary of the Synod of Bishops, 18 October 2015: http://w2.vatican.va/content/francesco/en/speeches/2015/october/documents/papa-francesco_20151017_50-anniversario-sinodo.html [Accessed 20/01/20].
2. Pope Francis, Address to participants in the plenary session of the Dicastery for the Laity, the Family and Life, 16 November 2019: http://w2.vatican.va/content/francesco/en/speeches/2015/october/documents/papa-francesco_20151017_50-anniversario-sinodo.html (not available in English) [Accessed 20/01/20].
3. See the conclusions of the Third General Conference of Latin American Bishops, Puebla, Mexico, 1979.
4. Final Document of the Special Synod on Amazonia, Chapter 1: 'The Amazon: From Listening to Integral Conversion': http://www.vatican.va/roman_curia/synod/documents/rc_synod_doc_20191026_sinodo-amazzonia_en.html [Accessed 20/01/20].
5. Barcelona Congress of the Ateneu Universtari Sant Pacià: 'La aportación del Papa Francisco a la teología y a la pastoral' (November 2019).

The Reform of the Roman Curia

AGENOR BRIGHENTI

In the reform of the Curia currently underway, Pope Francis is harnessing the winds that are blowing up from the southern hemisphere, freeing the Primacy from the eurocentricity that has characterised it, especially through the latter half of the last millennium. Within and around this process of reform, substantial changes are under way in how the Petrine ministry is exercised with implications for the make-up and profile of the College of Cardinals, as well as in the relationships between Local Churches and the Bishops' Conferences.

I Introduction

In Catholicism, the southern hemisphere Churches have maintained a secular resistance to the colonialism of former times and the neo-colonialism of today, rooted in eurocentricity and the principal cause of the centralist approach of the Roman Curia. With the election of Pope Francis, the winds that were blowing from the south brought the periphery into the centre of the Catholic Church, bringing with it a pressing need for urgent reform to ensure that the Church was really universal. From the first moments of his Pontificate, the "Pope who came from the end of the world", put in place a plan of substantial changes in the style and approach of the Papacy, in the exercise of the Petrine ministry and, particularly, in the make-up of the Roman Curia.[1] This had immediate implications for changes in the relationships between Local Churches and the Bishops' Conferences. In other words, it is necessary to place the primacy within Episcopal collegiality and in so doing at the heart of ecclesial synodality. The basis for this lies with the reforms arising from of the Second Vatican Council which conceived of the Church as a "Church of Churches" in which a one and undivided Church exists within Local Churches (*in quibus*), in communion with the other Churches (*ex quibus*).[2]

II Reforming the Curia: a cry from far away

The call for reform, which had come from afar, became clear in the Congregations of Cardinals which preceded the Conclave that elected the present Pope. Subsequently, in in his first Apostolic Exhortation, *Evangelii Gaudium*, he sealed this commitment: "I feel the need to move to a beneficial decentralisation" (EG 16). It is necessary, "to think as well of a conversion of the papacy"; "excessive centralisation, rather than helping, complicates the life of the Church and the dynamic of its mission" (EG 32).

The gradual process of centralisation of the Curia goes right back to the crisis of Conciliarism and the Counter Reformation of the Council of Trent, faced with the Protestant reforms at the dawn of the second half of the last millennium.

This centralisation reinforced ultramontanism, leading to the dogma of Papal infallibility, approved by the first Vatican Council in 1860,[3] outside the ecclesiological framework within which the *de Ecclesia* plan had originally been developed.[4] And, as it could not differ, the synodality of the Church was progressively compromised by the centralisation on Rome, especially as between the Church of Rome and the Dioceses, between the Bishop of Rome and the College of Bishops, in fact, between the Curia and the Local Churches, whether meeting as synods, or in the provincial councils from which the Episcopal Conferences would subsequently emerge.

III The reform of the Curia: an outstanding item of Vatican II renewal

The Second Vatican Council made profound changes right across the Church, although it left to the Pope the task of implementing them, especially so far as structural changes were concerned. Pope Paul VI tried hard but found himself held prisoner by the conservative wing that had been defeated in the Vatican Council but subsequently gained control of the Curia. Pope John Paul II also wanted to rethink the work of the Primacy, including seeking suggestions in his Encyclical *Ut Unum sint* – but without this leading to any concrete initiatives. The fact is that the Curia, despite the Vatican II reforms, continued on its path of increasing centralisation, becoming ever more a forum for the exercise of power than of service and also, to a certain extent, in its relations with the Pope. In recent decades the centralism of the Curia attained its highest levels. Scandals linked to power disputes, financial corruption and cover ups of cases of child abuse became almost commonplace during the primacy of Benedict XVI, factors not unconnected with the reasons that led him to step down as Pope.

The salvaging of ecclesial synodality by Vatican II, with its concept of the Church as the People of God ruled by a *sensus fidelium*, as well as the positioning of the Pope at the heart of the College of Bishops as a *primus inter pares*, brings right into question the centralism of the Curia. The concept of the Church of the second millennium, stemming from the existence of a supposed Universal Church, both preceding and taking place within the Local Churches, and of which the Pope is both representative and guarantor, is finally superceded. For the Council, there was no Church either above or apart from the Local Churches. The Local Church is an "integral" part (it shares in the whole) and not just a slice (a separate bit) of the catholic Church. The Church is a "Church of Churches" (Tillard). The one and undivided Church is manifest in the Local Churches (*in quibus*), in communion with the other Churches (*ex quibus*). This spells out clearly, the duty of care of the Bishop of a Local Church for the other Churches and places the exercise of his ministry at the heart of the Apostolic College and the Petrine ministry, presiding over the communion of the Churches as a *primus inter pares*.

IV The reforms of Pope Francis: the primacy of ecclesial synodality

The present reforms, carried out by Pope Francis, consist of no more than the implementation of the directives of Vatican II regarding the "structures of communion" within the Church.[5] As we have said, at the heart of this lies the necessity for a new approach to the Petrine ministry, one which also implies a reconfiguration of the Curia, of the Synod of Bishops, the College of Cardinals and the Bishops' Conferences. Regarding the College of Cardinals, the Pope is gradually moving it to a less Eurocentric, more universal profile building the presence it needs of the southern hemisphere Churches, where these days most Catholics are to be found.

With regard to the Synod of Bishops, the new Apostolic Constitution

The Reform of the Roman Curia

Episcopalis communion (18/09/2018) places this advisory body for the papacy at the "service of all People of God". It is making it a "channel better adapted to modern day evangelisation than to self-preservation" (n.1). From which, according to Pope Francis, comes the need for the Synod to be less about Bishops to "become increasingly a privileged instrument for listening to the People of God", made up as well of "people who do not hold episcopal office" (n.6). There still remains, nevertheless, the task of transforming the Synod into a body that is more deliberative than consultative, as well as the right of women to vote.

So far as the reform of the Curia itself is concerned, we need to wait for the publication of the New Constitution – *Praedicate Evangelium*, due to come out soon, which will replace the *Pastor Bonus* of 1988. The draft of the New Constitution was sent to the chairs of the National Bishops' Conferences, the Synods of the Eastern Churches, the Dicasteries of the Curia and to certain Pontifical Universities, requesting their feedback and suggestions. According to the working draft, the new profile for the Curia, in so far as an extended structure of the Primate's ministry, would take more into account from the other formal bodies with which it is linked such as the College of Cardinals, the Synod of Bishops, the Bishops' Conferences, together with Local Churches both in their autonomy and communion with all other Churches. And, as the College of Cardinals and the Synod of Bishops are linked more directly to serving the Petrine ministry, the Curia would become a body of support, and no longer of control, for the Bishops' Conferences and the Local Churches.[6] With this change the Bishops' Conferences would acquire far greater weight than they presently possess, including an authoritative role. Beyond this, the proposals indicate a profound change in the level of importance of the Dicasteries within the Curia. Contrary to the present roles where the Congregation of the Doctrine of the Faith has a visible pre-eminence relative to the other Dicasteries, those Congregations focusing on evangelisation, the promotion of development and peace, as well as those dedicated to the protection of the poor, are the ones that will come to the fore.

V How to get there

There are many who are impatient at the pace of Pope Francis' reforms. He is placing an emphasis on the process for delivering the results, above all in regard to the engagement and participation of the bodies that are involved. To move to synodality through an approach that is non-synodical, is to leave it entirely at the mercy of the good faith of those who will come in the future. Beyond assuring the legal and regulatory basis of the reforms, there is a need for a synodical conversation, since only by practising self-innovation can wider innovation be achieved.

Translated by Christopher Lawrence

Notes
1. Antonio Spadaro, A. 2013. "Intervista a Papa Francesco". *La Civiltà Cattolica*. September 19, 2013. Acesso em 12 de nov. 12 de 2014. https://w2.vatican. va/content/francesco/it/speeches/2013/ september/documents/papafrancesco_20130921_intervista-spadaro.html.
2. Cf. Hervé Legrand. The Roman Primacy, the communion between the Churches and the Communion between the bishops. *Concilium* 353 (2013/5), 71-86.
3. Cf. Norman. Tanner. Reform of the Curia through history. *Concilium* 353 (2013/5), 13-23.
4. Roger Aubert. *Vatican I, L'Orante*, Paris, 1964, page 247
5. Cf. Massimo Fagioli. Reform of the Curia in Vaticano II and subsequently. *Concilium* 353 (2013/5), 24-34.
6. Thomas J. Reese. Reforming the roman Curia. From an XVII court to a modern service. *Concilium* 353 (2013/5), 105-108.

In Memoriam of J.B. Metz

FRANCIS SCHÜSSLER FIORENZA

Johann Baptist Metz was born on 5 August 1928 in Auerbach in der Oberpfalz, a town in the Amberg-Sulzbach district of Bavaria, Germany. His death on December 2, 2019 in Münster, Germany marks the death of one of Germany's most influential Roman Catholic theologians of the post-World War II era. Metz was among the leading theologians who established *Concilium* as an international journal to further the reforms of Vatican II. In 1963, Metz was appointed Professor of Fundamental Theology on the Catholic Faculty of Theology at the University of Münster, in North-Rhine-Westphalia, Germany until his retirement in 1993.

Metz belongs to the post World War II generation of German theologians. As the war was ending, the German army increasingly lacked soldiers, Metz was drafted at the early age of sixteen. He was immediately sent to the front. A commander sent him with a message to bring to another commander. His way took him through an area that had been heavily bombed. Many of surrounding buildings were either on fire or destroyed by bombing. On his return Metz discovered that his camp was decimated by air attacks and found his fellow comrades dead. Soon after, he was captured and was shipped to the United States, where as a prisoner of war, he was sent to work on farms in Virginia and Maryland. In conversation with me, he remembered being so homesick those years and that the wife of the farmer felt sorry for him, since he was the youngest prisoner of war working on that farm in Virginia. She often made sure he had enough to eat. Despite the significance of these experiences, the impetus and tenor of Metz's theology stems not as much from his experience in the war itself as it does from his attempt to come to terms with the developments within German society, both religious and political society in the period leading up to the war. Where was the voice of the theologians? What role did the churches play? How do Christians deal with the Holocaust? It was the failures and crimes prior to the war that moved Metz to develop his political theology.

Metz began his academic studies at the University of Innsbruck with a philosophical dissertation on Martin Heidegger. As a student of Karl Rahner, he wrote a theological dissertation which published as *Christliche Anthropozentrik* in which he provided an interpretation of Thomas Aquinas that mirrored the roots of Rahner's anthropology in Aquinas. He edited the second edition of Karl Rahner *Hearers of the Word*, updating the lectures to reflect the further developments in Karl Rahner's theology in 1964. He was also the co-editor of a two volume Festschrift *Gott in Welt* published in honour of Karl Rahner. Metz and Karl Rahner remained in close friendship over the years. In many ways Karl Rahner was a "father figure" as well as a friend to Metz. His early writings reflect Rahner's theology, especially on anthropology and on the relation between church and society. Metz's friendship with Rahner continued even after started to develop his own voice in theology and in political theology and began to criticize elements of Rahner's transcendental philosophical approach.

As he began to teach fundamental theology at the University of Münster, he started to develop his initial conception of political theology as fundamental theology. This development took place in the context of the dialogues promoted by the Paulus Gesellschaft that aimed to bring West German philosophers, theologians, and scientists in dialogue with East German scientist and philosophers in dialogue.

Metz faced a specific critique of his theological position and political theology. As may be recalled, Metz sought to overcome not only what he saw as the weaknesses of the personalist, existentialist theologies of the time, but also the ecclesial failures during the era of National Socialism. His critics questioned whether his appeal to political theology could be understood as a return to the traditional domination of the church over the state and of theological views over society. Metz sought to avoid this criticism by emphasizing "an eschatological proviso" in his early articulation of political theology. He thus argued that political theology should not align itself with a specific government or system or institution because it would then lose its critical force to become an apologist of the status quo. Metz's emphasis on "the eschatological proviso" had the advantage of avoiding any future ideological defense of the political establishment, a perspective that was criticized by other political theologians like Jürgen Moltmann, Dorothee Söelle and Latin American liberation theologians.

Metz's conception of political theology has a consistency and yet shows a development as can be seen in his publications: *Faith in History and Society: Toward a Practical Fundamental Theology* (1997 German, 1980 English) *The Emergent Church: The Future of Christianity in a Postbourgeois World* (1980 German, 1987 English) with his later works *A Passion for God: The Mystical-Political Dimension of Christianity* (1998), in which he increasingly began to emphasize the role of memory.

He referred to the "dangerous memory" of the victims of suffering and injustice. He articulated the memory of suffering not only as central to understanding redemption, but also as a basic and fundamental category for his political theology, which he now called the "new political theology" in order to distance himself from Carl Schmitt's political theology and his anti-democratic, pro-Nazi, and anti-Semitic direction. Metz asserts that this memory of the suffering of Jesus and the suffering of other victims of injustice breaks through our prevailing consciousness. It mobilizes tradition as a critical and liberating force never to accept the societal status quo and always to have hope. This memory represents a theological understanding what it means to be a Christian community in discipleship of Jesus. The experience of suffering often cannot be traced back to an explicit guilt or history of guilt, but is an experience suffering and misery that cries out to God.

The Christian discourse of God, Metz argued, should be inspired by the mysticism of suffering unto God. Such discourse exhibits a poverty of spirit that does not immunize itself from the challenge that theodicy presents. But as discourse in a language of suffering and crisis, of doubt and danger, it raises that discourse to center of theology and it obligates us to more acutely perceive and attend to the suffering of others.

Metz was very much involved in the Würzburg Synod that sought to bring together all the German dioceses. East Germany refused to allow the dioceses within it to participate, so the synod was were limited to West Germany. Metz wrote a draft for the synod entitled "Our Hope: The Power of the Gospel to Configure the Future," in which he reemphasized the importance of focusing on the suffering of others and the victims of injustice. This prophetic stance is then linked to Christian hope. Christian hope is not a hope for a future that leaves behind the suffering and injustices of the past. The Christian community must live through the history of suffering to live out a history of hope. The religious crisis of the believers in the church itself must become acknowledged as a crisis that the church has to deal with.

One decisive point Metz maintained that the Catholic Church must acknowledge the holocaust and that the church had to take responsibility for it. The final document promulgated by the synod in 1975 *Our Hope: A Confession of Faith in this Time* took this impulse from Metz into account. It became the first official document in which the German Roman Catholic Church acknowledged the holocaust as a part of its history.

In remembering and honouring the legacy of Metz's contributions to theology, we should not overlook two characteristics of his writings. Many of them were more aphoristic than systematic, more evocative, and practical. He often authored small books that one might call "spiritual writings" but they are not so much pious as they underscore the central issues of Christian discipleship. *In Poverty of Spirit* (1968 English, 1962 German), Metz advocates also for the importance of an intellectual poverty as central to Christian discipleship. To be a Christian is not to know more than others, but to have an awareness of what we do not know. This poverty of spirit that enables one to hope in the face of the challenges and injustice of our world. It enables one to discard the intellectual superiority of spirit that cannot learn from others and their suffering. *In Followers of Christ: The Religious Life and the Church* (1977 German, 1978, English), Metz underscores that it is important for religious orders to exhibit discipleship through a memory that remembers injustice and the suffering of others and makes that essential to Christian discipleship.

Elisabeth and I were honoured to know Metz when we lived in Munster. One of our most cherished memories is that Metz officiated at our wedding, which Karl Rahner also attended. What I learned from Metz is a profound idea: the most dangerous memory for Christians (Jesus' suffering and death) is also Christianity's message of hope for the suffering of the world. Rest in Peace dear friend.

Francis Schüssler Fiorenza, Harvard University.

Contributors

RAÚL ZIBECHI is a popular educator and journalist born in Montevideo, Uruguay. He works with Latin American social movements on education and debate. He has published 20 books and hundreds of articles on collective action, including *Descolonizar el pensamiento crítico y las rebeldías* (2015). His latest book is *Nuevas derechas, nuevas resistencias* (2019).
   Address: Calle 20 de Septiembre 1454/008. Montevideo. 11600. Uruguay
   Email: raulzibechi@gmail.com

GINA MARCELA ÁRIAS RODRÍGUEZ has a degree in psychology from the Catholic University of Pereira and a master's degree in community psychology from the University of Chile. She has a doctorate in social and political sciences from the Ibero-American University in Mexico City. She teaches in the Catholic University of Pereira, where she is a member of the research group on communication and conflict. She is an activist with the Women's Peace Route.
   Email: gina.arias@ucp.edu.co

LUIS ADOLFO MARTÍNEZ HERRERA is a sociologist with a degree from the Universidad del Valle in Colombia. He has a master's degree in educational communication from the Technological University of Pereira and a doctorate in social sciences from FLACSO-Argentina. He lectures at the Catholic University of Pereira, where he is a member of the research group on communication and conflict. He is coordinator of the research programme on transitions, memories and violence.
   Email: luis.martinez@ucp.edu.co

GUSTAVO ESTEVA is a freelance public intellectual and social activist. He is the author of numerous books and essays and is a columnist for

Contributors

the Mexican daily La Jornada. He is a collaborator with the Universidad Centroamericana, the Centro de Encuentros y Diálogos Universitario and the Universidad de la Tierra in Oaxaca.

Address: Azucenas 610, Col. Reforma, Oaxaca, Oaxaca 68050, Mexico
Email: gustavoesteva@gmail.com

SUSAN ABRAHAM is Professor of Theology and Postcolonial Cultures, VP of Academic Affairs and Dean of Faculty at Pacific School of Religion. Ongoing research projects include issues in theological education and formation, interfaith and interreligious initiatives for social transformation, theology and political theory, religion and media, global Catholicism, and Christianity between colonialism and postcolonialism.

Address: Pacific School of Religion, 1798 Scenic Avenue, Berkeley, CA 94709.
Email: sabraham@psr.edu

SOFÍA CHIPANA QUISPE – Member of the Andean community of Theologians of Abya Yala and the Andean Theology Community (Peru-Argentina-Bolivia). She coordinates the Thakichañani Alternative Knowledge Center in El Alto de La Paz, Bolivia.

Address: Casilla 1191. La Paz, Bolivia.
Email: warmi_pacha@hotmail.com

CLEUSA CALDEIRA – Doctor in theology from the Jesuit faculty of Theology and Philosophy (FAJE). Currently doing a postgraduate in theology at FAJE. She exercises her pastoral ministry in the Igreja Presbiteriana Independente do Brasil. Scholarship recipient from CAPES (Coordenação de Aperfeiçoamento de Pessoal de Nível Superior, Brazil)

Address: Rua Amapá, 951- Centro. Paranavaí-PR-Brasil. CEP 87703-380
Email: cleucaldeira@gmail.com
ORCID: http://orcid.org/0000-0001-7202-0682

JOSÉ DE JESÚS LEGORRETA ZEPEDA is a professor and researcher in the Department of Religious Studies in the Universidad Iberoamericana in Mexico City, where he teaches courses in ecclesiology and sociology of religion at undergraduate and master's level. He has a doctorate in social

Contributors

science and politics from the Universidad Iberoamericana and a doctorate in systematic theology from the University of Granada in Spain. In recent years he has been coordinating a socio-ecclesial study exploring new forms of community in societies undergoing change.

Address: Universidad Iberoamericana, Ciudad de México. Prol. Paseo de la Reforma 880. Lomas de Santa Fe. 01219. Ciudad de México, Mexico.

Email: jesus.legorreta@ibero.mx

JUAN CARLOS LA PUENTE TAPIA works with individuals, groups, organisations and institutions in South and North America to enable their actions in favour of justice and peace to be rooted in work with those who are non-violently making cracks in and breaching the collusion with the various forms of oppression that bear down on themselves and others. Together with these groups he works to discern the wisdom that makes it possible to sustain hope, in communion with the ancestors whose lives offered and called for reconciliation. He is engaged in mutual support work through prayer and theology.

Address: 3339 SE Caruthers, Portland, OR 97214, USA

Email: jc.lapuente@yahoo.com

ALFREDO FERRO has a licenciate in philosophy from the Universidad Javeriana in Bogotá, a BA in theology from the Pontifical Catholic University (PUC) in Rio de Janeiro and an MA in sociology of religion from the PUC in São Paulo. Since 2014 he has been coordinator of the Jesuit Panamazonian Service of the conference of Latin American Jesuit provincials, based in Leticia, Colombia, the site of the triple border between Brazil, Peru and Colombia.

Address: Calle 10 No. 5-14, Leticia, Amazonas, Colombia

Email: alferrosj@gmail.com

AGENOR BRIGHENTI – Doctor of Religious and Theological Sciences, University of Louvain, Belgium, Professor of Theology, Pontifícia Universidade Católica, Curitiba, member of the Equipe de Reflexão Teológica do Conselho Episcopal Latino-americano (CELAM). Expert assessor for: Amazon Synod; the Brasil Bishops' Conference; the Aparecida Conference; the Latin American Episcopal Council's Conference at Santo Domingo. Author of over a hundred articles in national and international journals and dozens of books published in Brazil and overseas.

Address: Rua Servidão Guarani, 128, Bairro Tapera da Base, CEP 88049-270 FLORIANÓPOLIS, SC, Brasil

Email: agenor.brighenti@pucpr.br

FRANCIS SCHÜSSLER FIORENZA is the Stillman Professor of Roman Catholic Theological Studies at Harvard Divinity School. His primary interests are in the fields of fundamental or foundational theology, in which he explores the significance of contemporary hermeneutical theories as well as neo-pragmatic criticisms of foundationalism. His writings on political theology engage recent theories of justice, especially those of John Rawls and Jürgen Habermas, and have dealt with issues of work and welfare. He has also written on the history of nineteenth- and twentieth-century theology, focusing on both Roman Catholic and Protestant theologians. In addition to more than 150 essays in the areas of fundamental theology, hermeneutics, and political theology, his publications include the books *Foundational Theology: Jesus and the Church; Systematic Theology: Roman Catholic Perspectives*, edited with John Galvin; *Habermas, Modernity, and Public Theology*, edited with Don Browning; and *Modern Christian Thought, volume 2, The Twentieth Century*, written with James Livingston. He is presently completing a book entitled *Human Rights in the Crossfire: Political Theology Faces the Cultural Challenges to Rights*.

Address: Professor Francis Schüssler Fiorenza, Harvard Divinity School, 45 Francis Avenue, Cambridge, MA 02138

CONCILIUM
International Journal of Theology

FOUNDERS
Anton van den Boogaard; Paul Brand; Yves Congar, OP; Hans Küng;
Johann Baptist Metz; Karl Rahner, SJ; Edward Schillebeeckx

BOARD OF DIRECTORS
President: Thierry-Marie Courau OP
Vice-Presidents: Linda Hogan and Daniel Franklin Pilario CM

BOARD OF EDITORS
Susan Abraham, Los Angeles (USA)
Michel Andraos, Chicago (USA)
Mile Babic´ OFM, Sarajevo (Bosna i Hercegovina)
Antony John Baptist, Bangalore (India)
Michelle Becka, Würzburg (Deutschland)
Bernadeth Caero Bustillos, Osnabrück (Deutschland)
Catherine Cornille, Boston (USA)
Thierry-Marie Courau OP, Paris (France)
Geraldo Luiz De Mori SJ, Belo Horizonte (Brasil)
Enrico Galavotti, Chieti (Italia)
Margareta Gruber OSF, Vallendar (Deutschland)
Linda Hogan, Dublin (Ireland)
Huang Po-Ho, Tainan (Zhōnghuá Mínguó)
Stefanie Knauss, Villanova (USA)
Carlos Mendoza-Álvarez OP, Ciudad de México (México)
Gianluca Montaldi FN, Brescia (Italia)
Agbonkhianmeghe Orobator SJ, Nairobi (Kenya)
Daniel Franklin Pilario CM, Quezon City (Filipinas)
Léonard Santedi Kinkupu, Kinshasa (RD Congo)
João J. Vila-Chã SJ, Roma (Italia)

PUBLISHERS
SCM Press (London, UK)
Matthias-Grünewald Verlag (Ostfildern, Germany)
Editrice Queriniana (Brescia, Italy)
Editorial Verbo Divino (Estella, Spain)
EditoraVozes (Petropolis, Brazil)

Concilium Secretariat:
Couvent de l'Annonciation
222 rue du Faubourg Saint-Honoré
75008 – Paris (France)
secretariat.concilium@gmail.com
Executive secretary: Gianluca Montaldi FN

http://www.concilium.in

Concilium Subscription Information

April   **2020/2:** *Masculinities*

July   **2020/3:** *Theology, Power and Governance*

October   **2020/4:** *Signs of Hope for Muslim-Christian Dialogue*

December   **2020/5:** *Differently Able: for a Church Where All Belong*

February   **2021/1:** *Church in the Borders*

New subscribers: to receive the next five issues of Concilium please copy this form, complete it in block capitals and send it with your payment to the address below. Alternatively subscribe online at www.conciliumjournal.co.uk

Please enter my annual subscription for Concilium starting with issue 2020/2.

Individuals
____ £52 UK
____ £75 overseas and (Euro €92, US $110)

Institutions
____ £75 UK
____ £95 overseas and (Euro €120, US $145)

Postage included – airmail for overseas subscribers

Payment Details:
Payment can be made by cheque (£ Sterling only), by credit/debit card or bank transfer.
a. I enclose a cheque for £ _____ Payable to Hymns Ancient and Modern Ltd
b. To pay by Visa/Mastercard please contact us on +44(0)1603 785911 or go to www.conciliumjournal.co.uk
c. To pay in US $ or Euro € by bank transfer please contact us on +44(0)1603 785911

Contact Details:
Name ....
Address ....
....
Telephone .... E-mail ....

Send your order to *Concilium,* **Hymns Ancient and Modern Ltd**
13a Hellesdon Park Road, Norwich NR6 5DR, UK
E-mail: concilium@hymnsam.co.uk
or order online at www.conciliumjournal.co.uk

Customer service information
All orders must be prepaid. Your subscription will begin with the next issue of Concilium. If you have any queries or require Information about other payment methods, please contact our Customer Services department.

www.ingramcontent.com/pod-product-compliance
Ingram Content Group UK Ltd.
Pitfield, Milton Keynes, MK11 3LW, UK
UKHW040237250426
12048UKWH00042B/1558